THE DE PALMA CUT

LAURENT BOUZEREAU

DePALMA CUT

The Films of America's
Most Controversial Director

DEMBNER BOOKS • *New York*

DEMBNER BOOKS
Published by Red Dembner Enterprises Corp.,
80 Eighth Avenue, New York, N.Y. 10011

Distributed by W. W. Norton & Company, Inc.,
500 Fifth Avenue, New York, N.Y. 10110

Library of Congress Cataloging-in-Publication Data

Bouzereau, Laurent.
  The De Palma cut.

  Bibliography: p.
  Includes index.
  1. De Palma, Brian—Criticism and interpretation.
I. Title.
PN1998.3.D4B68   1988   791.43′0233′0924   88-7000
ISBN 0-942637-04-6

Excerpts from Brian De Palma's screenplays are used with the director's permission. Still photographs are from the author's private collection. All numbers, figures and grosses are from *Variety*.

Design by Antler & Baldwin, Inc.

To the memory of

Dominique Blanchion,
Elisabeth Courtland,
Carrie White,
Kate Miller,
Sally Bedina,
and
Gloria Revelle

CONTENTS

ACKNOWLEDGEMENTS

I am very grateful to Therese Eiben, my editor, whose notes, advice, kindness, enthusiasm, and respect helped me write *The De Palma Cut* to the best of my abilities. I want to thank Red Dembner for publishing my first book; Jim Byerley at HBO for making available to me a great deal of documentation and tapes of De Palma's films; Lois Mark for setting up my first interview with Brian De Palma; Kerri Bogda for helping me organize my notes; Monica Goldstein, Mr. De Palma's assistant; and my dear friend and agent, Kay McCauley.

I want to thank Alain Schlockoff from *L'Ecran Fantastique*, who launched my career as a film journalist.

I am grateful to the actors, directors, and writers whom I've interviewed through the years, and to all the publicists and agents who provided me with materials used in this book.

I thank my friends for encouraging my efforts and for giving me enough self-confidence to take on such challenges as this book.

I am in debt to my parents, Micheline and Daniel, to my sisters, Géraldine and Cécile, and to my family, whose support, love, and care have been of greatest help in my still young life and career.

I want to thank Mr. De Palma for authorizing some of the quotations in this book and for talking to me on several occasions . . . and for making movies worth writing about.

THE De PALMA CUT

He pulls a knife, you pull a gun;
he sends one of yours to the hospital,
you send one of his to the morgue.

> —Sean Connery as James Malone
> in *The Untouchables* on how
> to eliminate Al Capone.

I have a project called *Body
Double* and I'm going to make it
an 'X' movie. You wanna see violence? You wanna see sex? I think
it's about time to blow the top off
the ratings!

> —Brian De Palma
> on how to fight
> the rating system.

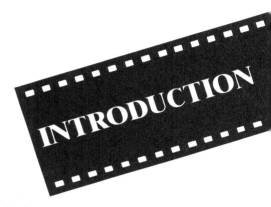

INTRODUCTION

Extreme Closeup
A straight razor moving back and forth across a razor strap.

Extreme Closeup
A straight razor shaving right cheek.

Extreme Closeup
A straight razor shaving upper and lower lips.

Extreme Closeup
A straight razor shaving left cheek.

Extreme Closeup
A straight razor shaving chin.

Extreme Closeup
A straight razor shaving throat.

Extreme Closeup
A straight razor shaving legs.

Extreme Closeup
A straight razor shaving right and left male breast.

11

Extreme Closeup
A straight razor shaving stomach.

Extreme Closeup
A straight razor shaving pubic hair.

Extreme Closeup
Eyes looking down.

Extreme Closeup
A straight razor trembling over naked pubic area.

Extreme Closeup
Eyes closing.

Extreme Closeup
A straight razor jerks down below frame.

Extreme Closeup
Eyes snap with shocked pain.

Extreme Closeup
Blood streams down hairless thighs.
                    —*Dressed to Kill.*
                        Original first scene,
                        written by Brian De Palma in 1979.

Filmmaking is an art form that manipulates the conscious as well as the subconscious minds of its audience. But because audiences often don't realize how rich the visual dialogue of certain directors can be, they passively watch their way from film to film. In most cases, moviegoers will recognize a director's artistic talent when his films "look nice," or are well photographed. Very seldom do filmgoers respond to a scene based on a director's ability to convey a story, and his characters' feelings, through his camera work. Audiences are not to be blamed for their lack of awareness. Very few contemporary directors truly employ the potential of the camera. With the constant evolution of the technical aspect of filmmaking, which has been developed to accommodate the growing demand for special effects, directors have become lazy. Some movies are so overwhelmingly full of tricks that when the smoke clears, it begins to seem to have been much ado about nothing. Very few directors are able to make a film compelling with the simple tools of a camera and an actor or two anymore.

Brian De Palma is a rare exception.

Persistently throughout his career, he's proved that he could convey plot and characterization with his camera alone. Most of his films have become cult classics and have marked important steps in film history, revolutionizing genres, breaking social and taboo issues, and challenging censorship.

Many of De Palma's critics call him the bastard son of Alfred Hitchcock. The analogies between the two directors mainly concern the similarities in plots and themes. While there's no denying that Hitchcock created a grammar for filmmaking, De Palma uses it with his own original style and language. De Palma declared in 1980:

> People sometimes address their interviews to what is Hitchcock in my movies as opposed to what is De Palma that isn't Hitchcock. I can rant and rave about other kinds of forms like split screens or slow motion that Hitchcock never used, but that's not the point. Dealing with Hitchcock is like dealing with Bach—he wrote every tune that was ever done. Hitchcock thought up practically every cinematic idea that has been used and probably will be used in this form.

Hitchcock was misunderstood in his own time. Now that his films are revered as classic examples of filmmaking, everyone seems to forget that, for example, *Psycho* (1960) was damned by the press, especially in England, as being "more miserable than the most miserable peepshows, and more suggestive than any pornographic film."

Hitchcock's genius has served as a model for many contemporary filmmakers, but it is Brian De Palma who is labelled an imitator. How often is Steven Spielberg asked where he got the idea of combining a zoom and a travelling shot on Roy Scheider when he witnesses a shark attack in *Jaws*? The answer is, of course, *Vertigo*. By dwelling upon the obvious references De Palma makes to Hitchcock, critics miss what is truly original in De Palma's work.

De Palma is Hitchcock's true successor. Willing to grapple with controversy, understanding the need to take risks, technically brilliant—De Palma does parallel Hitchcock in these categories—and one more—one other very important like-mindedness: De Palma knows that film is about visuals. Nobody working today can tell a story *with the camera alone* the way De Palma does.

*   *   *

In addition to being criticized for a lack of originality, Brian De Palma has been persistently attacked for being a misogynist. It is true that in many of De Palma's films, female characters are the victims of violence and perversity. But the reasons for this tendency are not as simple as they might appear.

Brian De Palma explains that, first of all, women are victims in his films for a logical reason: a woman's vulnerability is scarier to an audience than a man's. De Palma is merely following a perception established by society itself. De Palma once said in an interview that the reason why, for example, Robert Benton's thriller *Still of the Night* (1982) didn't frighten—nor attract—audiences was that Roy Scheider played the victim, and in people's minds, he was still the guy who killed the giant shark in *Jaws*!

Beyond this, De Palma's treatment of women is complex. His films focus on two particular groups of women: on one side, professional women who have decided to have a career and find themselves alone at the age of forty, and on the other side, bored housewives who inevitably feel inferior to their successful husbands. In both cases, the women begin to doubt their sexual potential. According to De Palma, their search for reassurance is dangerous and sometimes linked to death. The violence that befalls these women is perceived by De Palma's detractors as unfair and sexist punishment. The director's cold dissection of the American aristocracy (the victims in his films are most often rich, well-educated women) has earned him a bad reputation particularly among feminists.

But by dwelling upon the obvious, many critics and women fail to see that De Palma's films have explored women's roles and stereotypes through his female characters. In several of his films, De Palma transformed prostitutes into heroines. They take charge of situations and solve mysteries, while the aristocratic women remain victims. De Palma implies that prostitutes—who acknowledge and control their own sexuality—are less vulnerable to manipulation and danger than the insecure, confused, sexually frustrated housewives and career women.

For the sake of argument, one could also point to De Palma's view of men in his films, which is often highly critical. In *Dressed to Kill*, for example, the five male characters all contribute to a rather negative image of men in society. Michael Caine portrays Doctor Elliott, a respected and successful psychiatrist who is in fact a disturbed transsexual with murderous impulses. Keith Gordon plays Peter Miller, Angie Dickinson's son, a selfish teenager who cancels his date with his mother and later feels responsible for the incidents that lead to her death. Dennis Franz is a sleazy, vulgar, and insensitive detective. Ken Baker plays the seductive man who picks up Angie Dickinson at a museum and has sex with her despite evidence that he knows he has a venereal disease. Fred Weber, who portrays Dickinson's husband, is perhaps the worst of them all. His self-serving performance in bed leads his frustrated wife to doubt her sexual worth—he encourages her promiscuity, and is, in a sense, responsible for her death.

According to De Palma's portrayal of his male characters, the man often pushes the woman to commit desperate and dangerous acts. This, too, helps to explain De Palma's positive portrayal of prostitutes—such as Nancy Allen in *Dressed to Kill*. Logically, prostitutes know that, more than women, men are weak and vulnerable.

In 1987, the critics recognized Adrian Lyne's *Fatal Attraction*—in which a woman (Glenn Close) terrorizes her married lover (Michael Douglas)—as a compelling statement on anonymous sex. Reviewers largely ignored the fact that *Fatal Attraction* also presents a misogynistic and sexist view of women. In the film, Michael Douglas is caught between a boring, castrative wife (Anne Archer), and a psychotic lover, (Close).

The critics have been less generous toward De Palma—in their obsession with his perceived hostility toward women, they have overlooked many of the important messages of his films.

All this controversy pales in light of De Palma's visual brilliance. But the intensity of the attacks on De Palma have led the director to make films like *Body Double* (1984), with the express purpose of revolting critics and women even more. De Palma also intentionally projects an image that matches the controversy over his personality. To the question "What do you do for fun?" he answered, "I strangle children in the park!" Often bad judgment in choosing his themes have distracted De Palma from what he really does brilliantly and that is to trust his visual concepts to establish the elements in his films.

The De Palma Cut explores De Palma's themes and visual techniques, and studies the director's work from many angles—including projects that never came to fruition, but served as links in De Palma's evolving filmic philosophy.

This book has one goal: to affirm that Brian De Palma is a gifted visionary director, and that his craft and his approach are highly original. All of De Palma's visual concepts, combined with his fascination with themes such as voyeurism, sexuality, guilt, and the double, make his work unique, and worthy of examination.

ONE

When asked about his childhood, Brian De Palma answers: "See *Home Movies;* it's all in there." And indeed, Brian De Palma's personality is revealed through his films. In *Home Movies* (1979) and *Dressed to Kill* (1980), De Palma describes himself, through the characters played by Keith Gordon, as an introverted, misunderstood, lonely, but intelligent teenager.

Though his first passion was for math, technology, and electronics, De Palma gradually moved away from science; he had owed his interest to his father, a successful orthopedic surgeon, who would have loved to see his son take after him. But De Palma discovered that his future was in film rather than in the scientific field, and a gap grew between father and son. In consequence, young Brian felt rejected by his father, who did not approve of his choice to become a director.

As a result, De Palma's early films reveal sharply critical views of science and the medical profession. In *Sisters* (1973), De Palma condemns science and the medical profession for being imperfect and too vulnerable to human error. *Sisters* is the story of a doctor who falls in love with a Siamese twin and performs an unsuccessful surgery, which causes the death of one sister and triggers a split personality complex in the other. What De Palma discloses is that there is no perfection in science because feelings inevitably get in the way; science to him is a selfish passion that tries to prevent the practical and logical mind from being simply human. Similarly, in *Dressed to Kill*, Keith Gordon portrays a teenager so involved in his science project that he thoughtlessly cancels his date with his mother (played by Angie Dickinson). It is he who, in fact, permits her hidden sexual desires to come out—she picks up a stranger at a museum, and later meets with death.

Brian De Palma establishes in both films that science can have fatal and unmanageable consequences. With moviemaking, however, he discovered a kind of power not accessible through science. By mastering the art of manipulation, he found a way of being in control by throwing audiences out of control. . . .

Brian De Palma was born on September 11, 1940, in Newark, New Jersey. When he was five, he moved with his family to Philadelphia. Though his parents were of Italian descent and were Catholic, he went to a Presbyterian school and was not exposed to Italian-American culture (as was his contemporary Martin Scorsese, who was raised in Manhattan's Little Italy). Brian De Palma was the youngest of a family of three boys. De Palma always felt dominated by his older brothers, Bruce and Barton, and his inferiority complex was encouraged by his mother, who only had eyes for them. De Palma once claimed he could be on the cover of *Time* magazine without her noticing it. Mrs. De Palma did not work, though her secret ambition was to become a singer. ("Your mother sang?" a journalist once asked De Palma. He answered, "Only in her head!")

During his early years, De Palma experienced an event that left with him a sensation of intense terror: his two brothers were playing and young Brian hid behind a refrigerator and got stuck; eventually, he had to cry out for help. Evidently, this event reinforced the inferiority complex De Palma felt toward his brothers, and added to it the fear of being humiliated for losing control.

In *Body Double* (1984) Jake Scully (Craig Wasson) relates this story and reveals that the fear De Palma experienced as a boy never quite left his subconscious. Scully is in an acting class and, after disclosing an embarrassing childhood experience, loses his concentration and starts to cry. The killer (Gregg Henry) assists in the session, perceives Scully's vulnerability, and concludes that he has found the perfect witness to the murder of his wife:

JAKE
I remember that it was dark, really black and I was just a little kid. The wall behind me was cold and damp. I was hiding. I was part of this game Sardine, and I was It. I was hiding and everybody was

looking for me. I was behind the freezer in the basement and I had jammed myself so hard behind it that I couldn't move. I'm afraid . . .

DRAMA TEACHER

What are you afraid of?

JAKE

That they're not going to find me.

DRAMA TEACHER

But they're not supposed to find you.

JAKE

But I'm afraid because I can't move.

DRAMA TEACHER

Why don't you cry out?

JAKE

I can't, I'm afraid; besides, I'm the Sardine and they're not supposed to find me.

DRAMA TEACHER

Who can't find you?

JAKE

My brothers. They're bigger than me and that's the first time they ever let me play.

DRAMA TEACHER

If they're your brothers, they'll want to help you, right?

JAKE

No. No, they'll never let me play again.

DRAMA TEACHER

They're bigger than you are, aren't they?

                              JAKE

Yeah . . .

                          DRAMA TEACHER

Will they hurt you?

                              JAKE

Yes . . .

                          DRAMA TEACHER

How?

                              JAKE

They'll laugh at me for getting stuck behind the freezer and for
crying out for help . . .

Jake Scully resolves the conflicts of his personality by acting out his
fears. De Palma himself probably found in directing his own way to release
his anger and frustration and get the attention he had never received as a child.
Of course, this explains why De Palma chose to add shock value to most of
his films—to keep people's eyes riveted to them. De Palma is almost like an
enfant terrible, ready to turn to the most outrageous themes in order to attract
attention.

When he was seventeen, Brian De Palma wrote a thesis entitled "The
Application of Cybernetics to the Solution of Differential Equations," for
which he received a gold medal at the Delaware Valley Scientific Fair, and
also the second prize at the National Scientific Congress of Los Angeles. It
seemed evident then that Brian De Palma was successful enough to be
destined for a fruitful scientific career. He was motivated in his research by
the ambitions of Bruce, the eldest child, and by his father's encouragement
and support.

By the age of sixteen, De Palma had developed a high tolerance for
blood—and certainly a fascination for it, since it has been liberally poured
into his films—by witnessing his father and his colleagues performing
surgery.

Brian De Palma studied physics and technology at Columbia University
in New York. It was during those years that he saw Alfred Hitchcock's *Vertigo*
(1958) and discovered the art of filmmaking. He had studied photography
with his brother Barton (who later did some photographic work on *Hi, Mom!*
[1970] and the painting of Genevieve Bujold and Cliff Robertson in *Obsession*

[1976]. But with *Vertigo*, De Palma suddenly realized that film could be an intellectual game. De Palma understood that Hitchcock manipulated his audience and conveyed his plot through complex and clever visuals. He discovered that directing meant power and control. Filmmaking had suddenly become more precise than science itself.

De Palma's decision to abandon the scientific field for directing angered his father, but despite his lost of paternal support, De Palma quickly found a community elsewhere. He created a film association between Columbia University and Sarah Lawrence College. The famous stage director Wilford Leach, who conducted a theater class at Sarah Lawrence, was immediately impressed by the young man's energy and interest in filmmaking. Leach soon became De Palma's mentor. According to De Palma, Leach was one of the very few people who ever understood him. (Later, he would acknowledge the influence of his teacher by naming the character played by William Finley, the hero of *Phantom of The Paradise*, Winslow Leach.)

After finishing his studies at Columbia, De Palma transferred to Sarah Lawrence College for two years. It was during this time that he began to direct short films. In 1960, Brian De Palma made *Icarus,* which he today considers a pretentious film, though he admits that it encouraged him to learn more. At first, De Palma was only supposed to be the cameraman on *Icarus,* but the director left the set after many arguments with De Palma, who was already trying to impose his own visual ideas, regardless of his position. Luckily, De Palma was then offered the opportunity to finish the film himself. *Icarus* was shot in 16mm with a secondhand Bolex camera De Palma had bought for $150.00 with the money from his scholarship.

He invested the money he had received from science awards into making another short film entitled *660124, The Story of an IBM Card. 660124* is the story of a painter who loses his life to the benefit of his art. It reveals a more sophisticated style than *Icarus*, since logically De Palma had improved his skill from his still-fresh experience on his first short.

At this time, De Palma was a good friend of several young filmmakers, including Martin Scorsese. De Palma's approach was less film-oriented than that of Scorsese, who had studied cinematic history and become a walking film encyclopedia. De Palma could hardly be mistaken for a film buff, despite the admiration for the French New Wave that greatly influenced his style. The New Wave generated interest because it represented a community, whose most memorable founders were François Truffaut, Jean Luc Godard, and Claude Chabrol. Their goal was to create a different cinema that, without necessarily being controversial, had a new style. The style came from the directors' creativity as well as from the their low budgets, which forced them to innovate and to uncover new visual concepts. Toward the end of the sixties, De Palma wanted to bring to the American cinema what the New Wave had brought to the French film industry. Therefore, De Palma almost immediately established himself as a rebel against the Hollywood movie community—a community that believed only in profit, rather than in allowing directors to express themselves freely through their art. Thus, many of De Palma's early films were modelled on a very avant-garde visual style—for example, many shots were filmed with a hand-carried camera, giving them a documentary-like flavor, which implies that fiction is often close to reality.

In 1962, De Palma received the Rosenthal Foundation Award, for the best short film directed by a filmmaker under twenty-five, for *Wonton's Wake*. In this film, William Finley, who would faithfully work on many of De Palma's films later in his career, plays a mad artist who falls in love with one of his sculptures. One night, the statue turns into a woman and escapes. Finley desperately chases her. De Palma was awarded $1000 for *Woton's Wake*, and at last found the energy and the confidence to do a more ambitious project, a feature film called *The Wedding Party*.

THE WEDDING PARTY *(1964/1966, released in 1969)*

> SYNOPSIS: In two days, Charlie (Charles Pfluger) will marry Josephine Fish (Jill Clayburgh) on her family's estate. Upon his arrival with his two best friends, Cecil (Robert De Niro) and Alistair (William Finley), Charlie doesn't receive the attention he expected; his future in-laws completely ignore his presence and Josephine is constantly under the surveillance of her conservative grandmother. When Charlie discovers that Josephine has their future all planned out in the most old fashioned way, he decides to run away. Cecil and Alistair catch Charlie and bring him back to his bride in time for the ceremony.

The Wedding Party was a collaborative effort of Wilford Leach, Brian De Palma, and Cynthia Munroe, a wealthy film student who invested $100,000 into the making of the film.

Originally, Munroe wanted Leach to direct the film, but he ended up working exclusively with the actors and left the shooting and editing to

De Palma. The film starred newcomers Jill Clayburgh, Jennifer Salt, and Robert De Niro. De Palma knew that the screenplay he had co-written with Leach and Munroe presented—purposely and for budgetary reasons—a modest, unsophisticated plot. In order to make up for the dullness of the subject, De Palma decided to give *The Wedding Party* an unconventional visual style—his use, for example, of both slow and fast motion almost suggests that the normal and deliberately boring characters are lost in the middle of a Chaplin-like burlesque comedy. Most of the actors were still students, and the trio decided to allow the cast to improvise most of the scenes, again following a tradition established by the French New Wave. This method helped to give the film an amateurish quality that seemed intentional and charming.

The making of *The Wedding Party* took two years. During that time, De Palma directed other shorts, including *Jennifer* (1964) with Jennifer Salt, and *Mod* (1964), a segment on The Who and the Rolling Stones that was intended as part of a feature-length documentary that was never completed. In 1965, Brian De Palma shot, in New Orleans and in several other southern cities, a film sponsored by the National Association for the Advancement of Colored People (NAACP) entitled *Bridge That Gap*, and in 1966, he did *Show Me a Strong Town and I'll Show You a Strong Bank* for the Treasury Department. That year, De Palma also directed a documentary on the opening of an exhibit at the Museum of Modern Art in New York, called *The Responsive Eye*. Instead of making a conventional nonfiction film, De Palma proved, by filming the people who attended the event, that the "show" was not only on the walls.

Munroe, Leach, and De Palma had many arguments during the making of *The Wedding Party*, which was finally completed in 1966. De Palma had fights about the budget of the film with Munroe, and differences with Leach primarily over the lead actor, Charles Pfluger. De Palma hated the young man's work—his interpretation of Charlie was, according to the director, too shallow. Leach disagreed. The conflicts didn't alter the friendship between the two men or the respect they had for one another, but their frequent arguments led Leach to comment that De Palma was one of the very few artists he knew who said: "The world is wrong, the critics are wrong and I am right!" (De Palma has retained this attitude, and it probably explains his many conflicts with the press.)

De Palma organized screening after screening of *The Wedding Party*, trying to find a distributor, but his efforts were not rewarded. Leach, Munroe, and he ended up financing the release. *The Wedding Party* received two favorable reviews, one mixed, and three negative. The *New York Daily News* wrote *"The Wedding Party* has style, charm and humor galore. It's a pleasure to see!" "As newcomers to the feature film field, the independent team of Miss Munroe, Mr. Leach and Mr. De Palma are welcome. They have created something fresh and funny," said Howard Thompson in the *New York Times*. *Variety* was less enthusiastic and wrote, "one suspects that the various techniques were either used to cover an absence of content, or that the techniques themselves were deemed more fundamental than ideas of substance." This last review failed to take into account that *The Wedding Party* could not be perceived as a conventional feature; it was a student film— or more exactly, a film made by students, experimenting and testing their abilities to make a feature-length movie. *The Wedding Party* was nothing more than a crude sketch of what De Palma had yet to show.

MURDER A LA MOD (1967)

> SYNOPSIS: *Murder a la Mod* is an erotic thriller that shows the murder of an actress repeatedly stabbed in the eyes with an ice pick from three different points of view. The first segment adopts a structure similar to a soap opera. The second is an eerie Hitchcock-like episode. And the film ends in the spirit of a burlesque comedy, in which William Finley plays a deaf-mute actor.

Murder a la Mod (no connection with De Palma's short entitled *Mod*) was a project over which De Palma had total control. With it, he explored for the first time the horror genre, which officially became his field with and after *Sisters. Murder a la Mod* goes beyond experimentation, and can be considered as a "style exercise"—De Palma used the device of a film within a film to draw parallels between fiction and reality, and to confuse the audience. The film also makes references to Hitchcock, although De Palma chose to close the film with black humor, implying that he could build up suspense and then, in the end, get a good laugh out of it.

De Palma was able to do *Murder a la Mod* thanks to the collaboration of two of his college roommates Jared Martin and Ken Burrows. In addition to being involved with the production, both men acted in the film—Martin played a producer and Burrows a director.

Retrospectively, De Palma thought that *Murder a la Mod* had a bad screenplay (written by him) which made the plot confusing and unconvincing.

It seems surprising that the criticism came directly from the mouth of the director himself. De Palma had been motivated to make the film by a desire to explore various genres and have fun with his camera. But—as he later realized—he had failed to add substance to his ideas. Slowly, De Palma was establishing himself as a visual director rather than as a great storyteller.

Murder a la Mod played for two weeks in New York City only, in a double feature with Paul Bartel's *Secret Cinema*. De Palma's second feature went totally unnoticed.

GREETINGS (1968)

> SYNOPSIS: Three friends of draft age are desperately trying to prove they're the wrong candidates to fight in Vietnam. While waiting for the Army's verdict, the three men continue living out their obsessions: Lloyd (Gerrit Graham) is consumed by his morbid fascination with President Kennedy's assassination; Paul (Jonathan Worden) pursues an apprenticeship in lovemaking by meeting his female partners through a computer dating service; and Jon (Robert De Niro) is a voyeur who has decided to live his wildest fantasies. Finally, only Jon is sent to Vietnam, and when American television interviews him in action, he simply asks a Vietnamese girl to strip in front of the camera.

The title of De Palma's next film, *Greetings*, was a good omen. It brought him commercial acceptance and critical attention, and allowed him to solidly establish himself as a leader among the New York avant-garde directors.

Greetings marked the first collaboration between producer Charles Hirsch and Brian De Palma. Fascinated by filmmaking, Hirsch had made several short films before he discovered that he was a more effective producer than director. Hirsch started in the film industry as a theater manager and booker, and was later put in charge of finding talented new directors for Universal Pictures. He screened short films and then recommended to the studio the most promising young directors, to be considered for a feature-length film. It was through this channel that Hirsch met De Palma. Hirsch, who was then twenty-six, was getting more and more frustrated with the studio's attitude toward young directors, and he let De Palma convince him to move on to less restrictive opportunities.

Greetings was Hirsch's idea. De Palma developed the characters, who were based on himself and Hirsch. The voyeur and the man haunted by the assassination of Kennedy were drawn from De Palma, and the young man obsessed with sex, as well as the madness of the Gerrit Graham character were drawn from Hirsch. The dialogue was written during rehearsals in collaboration with the actors, some of whom were students at Columbia University. The cast also included Robert De Niro, Gerrit Graham, Rutanya Alda and William Finley—by now a perennial in the De Palma *oeuvre*. There were eight nonunion crew members, either friends of De Palma and Hirsch or film students. Hirsch financed *Greetings* thanks to $20,000 of credit on $1,000 cash, extended by a lab for film processing. Hirsch then hit on his parents, sold his Bolex camera, and found two investors to whom he promised large percentages (neither he nor his parents received anything on the gross of the film).

Greetings was shot for $15,000 cash and the rest was all deferred. The total cost of the film was $43,100, which included about $4,000 wasted before Hirsch and De Palma realized that 16mm film would limit the release to very few art houses, and decided to change format. The editing of *Greetings* was rapid since most scenes had been filmed in one shot.

With *Greetings*, De Palma's style began to take shape; he was confirming the fact that he gave priority to visual concepts over a substantial plot. More than just a story, *Greetings* is a thematic film about the Vietnam era and how it was received in America by youth and the media. As he would continue to do throughout his career, De Palma made up for lack of substance in the script of *Greetings* with strong, shocking elements and sophisticated camera movements. He also developed his art of manipulating the audience by inserting surprisingly erotic scenes that caused the film to get an X rating. Such methods have caused many critics to point out the gratuitous elements in De Palma's films. But in fact, rather than being gratuitous, De Palma's erotic scenes are deliberately manipulative and therefore serve a specific purpose. Likewise, the complicated camera movements, which gradually become a tradition for De Palma, are an intentional part of his effort to use a visual language over a conventional dialogue and structure.

When the distribution company SIGMA III offered a deal to De Palma and Hirsch, they jumped at the chance. SIGMA III received eighty percent of the grosses; Hirsch and De Palma had no idea that *Greetings* would make at the box office three times what it had cost. The reviews were mixed, but all the critics acknowledged De Palma's visual insight, which was after all the director's primary concern. William Bayer wrote, in the *New York Times*,

"De Palma shows talent and the intimation of an original style in his handling of actors and the ingenuity of his framing." *Greetings* became a cult movie, and was called "an overground sex-protest film" by Archer Winsten of the *New York Post*. The film played at New York's 34th Street East theater, and the ads read: "Don't miss this year's miracle on 34th Street!"

After the success of *Greetings*, the president of Filmways Pictures, Martin Ransohoff, offered De Palma and Hirsch a contract to do a sequel originally titled *Son of Greetings*, which later became *Hi, Mom!* But before *Hi, Mom!* went into production, De Palma made a documentary on the controversial play *Dionysus in '69*.

DIONYSUS IN '69 (1969)

> SYNOPSIS: *Dionysus in '69* is a split-screen documentary film on the scandalous, critically and socially controversial play created by Richard Schechner, based on Euripides' *The Bacchae*, and performed by the Performance Group.

Dionysus in '69 was created by the members of the Performance Group (to which William Finley belonged) under the direction of Richard Schechner, who brought a new erotic dimension to the ancient Greek classic *The Bacchae*. The group's intention was to explore the theatrical language, and for over a year audiences came to the Performance Group's garage in Greenwich Village to see the play and to be in it. The spectators were invited to participate in the death ritual of the young king Pentheus (William Finley). Members of the troupe, and occasionally of the audience, stripped and performed bizarre body movements to undergo symbolic sacrifice. The play was acclaimed, disparaged, and argued about. Obviously, the play was manipulating the audience by transforming the spectators into voyeurs and inviting them to participate in sexually-oriented rituals. Of course, what appeared to some as a highly intellectual experience was assailed by others as an invitation to group sex.

Dionysus in '69 received a Village Obie Award as well as a prize at the 1969 Belgrade International Theatre Festival. The controversy lived on when the entire cast was arrested for indecent exposure after a successful performance at the University of Michigan.

William Finley helped Brian De Palma convince Richard Schechner to let him film a live performance. De Palma filmed the play with three cameras;

he shot the action itself, and the cameras of Bruce Rubin (who had written De Palma's short, *Jennifer*) and Robert Fiore concentrated on the reactions of the audience. The film was presented as a triptych on the screen—with the views of all three cameras shown simultaneously. Despite the fact that *Dionysus in '69* didn't get the notice De Palma expected (he should have guessed that people would go to a performance rather than going to see the play on film), it today reveals its strong influence on the development of the director's visual style. The split-screen device became one of his trademarks. Also, some of the shots of the sacrifices of the king in *Dionysus* are identical to those in *Carrie* (1974), when Sissy Spacek is showered with pig's blood, as well those in *Sisters* (1973), when, after killing William Finley, Margot Kidder holds his blood-covered hands. De Palma's film of *Dionysus in '69* ultimately preserved the Performance Group's attempt to revive Euripides' classic, and immortalized a step in theater history that would not have lived on without it.

HI, MOM! (1970)

> SYNOPSIS: Jon (Robert De Niro), the voyeur from *Greetings*, is back. This time, he is determined to make a living off his obsession. He convinces a producer (Allen Garfield) to lend him money to make a candid-camera porno movie on the private lives of his neighbors. Despite all his efforts, Jon's career as a filmmaker is brief. He switches goals, and is engaged to play a cop by a troupe of militants who have created a seminar called "Be Black Baby," in which white people experience racial oppression by pretending to be black. Finally, Jon decides to settle down with Judy (Jennifer Salt), the young woman he used to peep on. Quickly, Jon is bored with his normal life, and he destroys his building with dynamite. Jon comes back to the scene of his crime and is interviewed on television; he protests against violence and also takes the opportunity to say "hi" to his mother.

Brian De Palma got the basic idea for *Hi, Mom!* when he watched the long lines of people waiting to see *Greetings*—he noticed a building near the theater, and wondered what was going on behind each window. The film is a look at post–Vietnam War America, including its relationship to discrimination against black people.

The segment of the film entitled "Be Black, Baby" was shot in 16mm (later blown up to 35mm) and in black and white, to set the episode apart from the rest of the movie. Most of the scenes in *Hi, Mom!* were rehearsed before the shooting, but many were improvised on the set. Actress Rutanya Alda recalls:

> *Hi, Mom!* was an adventure. My twenty-minute "Be Black, Baby" sequence in the film was improvised, very theatrical and very demanding. It was a one-take sequence. We worked things out and then went for it. The dress I wore was my own; it was ruined at the end of the film—I played the rape victim. On a low budget like this one, I didn't bother getting reimbursed; I just threw it away!

Greetings, as well as *Hi, Mom!*, was made outside film union regulations. The hours were long, and the pay was low for both cast and crew.

Once the shooting was over, De Palma found *Hi, Mom!* too scattered. There were basically three different movies in one: the adventures of Jon the voyeur, the "Be Black, Baby" segment, and the relationship between Jon and Judy. De Palma admitted to being slightly disappointed with the end results. What had happened with *Hi, Mom!* was the typical situation of a film failing to live up to its prequel. *Hi, Mom!* was neither as clever nor as interesting as *Greetings*, despite an excellent set-up and the originality of the "Be Black, Baby" segment—which seemed, unfortunately, completely out of place.

Charles Hirsch thought he had on his hands an off-beat version of *The Graduate* (1967), and he decided to get exhibitors to show the film in big theaters rather than release it in art movie houses, where it truly belonged. De Palma disagreed; he knew that despite the humor in the film, *Hi, Mom!* was still an underground movie made for a select audience.

The cast of *Hi, Mom!*, which included Robert De Niro, Jennifer Salt, and Gerrit Graham, got great reviews, and so did De Palma. The film was described as "Hilarious," and "Uproarious." Richard Schickel wrote in *Life* magazine that *Hi, Mom!* had an "enormous exuberance," and according to Paul Zimmerman of *Newsweek*, the film had "the right blend of savagery and humor." The "Be Black, Baby" segment was received as a raw, powerful, and devastating sequence: "The episode is tense, electric, and terrifying," said *Time* magazine; "It's harrowingly and appallingly funny!" wrote *Women's Wear Daily*. But strangely enough, the audience seemed to agree with De Palma's disappointment rather than with the enthusiasm of the critics, and *Hi, Mom!* failed financially at the box office. De Palma felt so frustrated at the time that he wanted to move away from doing social satires—he even talked about doing a 3-D movie! But Warner Brothers and Hollywood were calling him. De Palma couldn't refuse the offer, and agreed to direct a comedy entitled *Get To Know Your Rabbit*.

GET TO KNOW YOUR RABBIT *(1970; released in 1972)*

SYNOPSIS: Donald Beeman (Tom Smothers) is an employee of the rich, powerful and tyrannical Mr. Turnbull (John Astin). Frustrated with his job and his miserable existence, Donald decides to become an itinerant tap-dancing magician, following intensive training with the eccentric Mr. Delasandro (Orson Welles). Donald meets a "terrific-looking-girl" (Katharine Ross), falls in love, and enjoys his freedom until one day he crosses the path of his ex-boss, Mr. Turnbull, who has become a poor alcoholic. Donald's magic routine with a rabbit gives Turnbull the idea to exploit this concept as a kind of relaxation for powerful businessmen. Turnbull becomes rich and again turns his back on Donald, who, disgusted, simply decides to make himself disappear.

Brian De Palma, unlike most of the "movie brats," had always wanted to be regarded as a New York director. He refused to have anything to do with the studios and considered Hollywood merely a marketplace. After his experience on *Get To Know Your Rabbit*, his hatred and disdain for the Hollywood establishment finally became justified.

Warner Brothers desperately wanted to work with East Coast–based directors, and expected them to bring to their films a new and "artistic" look. *Get To Know Your Rabbit* was a comedy and a satire that Jordan Crittenden had written for the famous stand-up comedian Tommy Smothers. At the beginning of production, Smothers realized that his director wasn't used to the politics that ruled a big studio, and offered De Palma all his support. But gradually, the relationship between the two men fell apart. Both De Palma and Smothers were insecure about the project. *Rabbit* was the director's first film in Hollywood and he was not used to being controlled by a studio. Smothers was making his film debut and considered *Rabbit* a turning point in his career that would either make him or break him as a star. Smothers tried to pressure De Palma and became dictatorial, and the disputes affected the quality of the scenes. Warner was very unhappy with the dailies; in fact, the only scenes that worked well were the ones that starred Orson Welles.

Welles had been brought in the picture to give it "star quality." He had told De Palma: "Tell me what to do, don't bother me, and let me get out of here as fast as possible!" Never before having been directed by such a young director (De Palma was thirty), Welles refused to learn his dialogue and wanted to have it written on large boards (cue sheets) in front of him so he could read his lines during the takes—he argued with De Palma that this was the way Marlon Brando liked to work. Finally, De Palma won the battle and Welles gave in and learned his lines. Welles gradually came to respect De Palma because, despite his inexperience, he knew how to stand up for himself and to stick to his ideas, even when they put his contract with Warner in jeopardy. Also, Welles had been in a similar position throughout his own career, and could only appreciate someone like De Palma, who stood alone against the star of the film and one of the most important Hollywood studios. At the end of the shooting, the two men were close friends, and Welles tried to support De Palma when he was fired by Warner.

The conflicts on the set had slowed down the schedule and Warner could not get rid of Smothers unless they were willing to reshoot the entire production. So De Palma was replaced by Peter Nelson, a "project coordinator," who shot some additional footage. Warner also decided to change De Palma's ending. Originally, there was a dramatic twist during which Smothers slaughtered a rabbit on television in order to ruin his ex-boss, who had stolen his idea. The killing of the rabbit was in fact a magic trick. Instead, in the film, Smothers simply makes himself disappear.

Rabbit slept on the shelves for two years after it was completed; Smothers was convinced it would hurt his career if the movie were released. When *Get To Know Your Rabbit* finally came out in 1972, the critics forgave De Palma for his faux pas, and concluded that his New York sensibility didn't jive with the Hollywood mentality. They knew that there was a big difference between the way they made movies on the West Coast and the way directors were treated in New York. New York, like Europe, allowed its filmmakers more freedom; Hollywood had a tendency to abuse directors by controlling the movies' editing and by interchanging directors on the same film as had been the case with *Rabbit*. Hollywood ignored the fact that the soul of a movie was its director, not the money behind it.

Brian De Palma felt betrayed, bitter, and deeply hurt by the whole experience. All his suggestions to the studio had been turned down. Though Vincent Canby wrote in the *New York Times* that he was convinced "De Palma would one day make a very good American comedy," the director came back to New York, ready for a change. Brian De Palma had entered the second period of his career. His red period.

THE DePALMA CUT

Two

What Brian De Palma was looking for after his disastrous experience on *Get to Know Your Rabbit* was certainly not the comedy, *Fuzz*, which United Artists wanted him to do. *Fuzz* was based on a best seller by Ed McBain, and De Palma might have considered the project if it hadn't already seemed out of control. The New York film crews were on strike and United Artists planned to shoot the film at the MGM studios, although *Fuzz* took place in Manhattan. Since the frantic city was one of the main ingredients in the story, De Palma felt that making the film in a studio would spoil its appeal. Also, he didn't think that Yul Brynner and Raquel Welch, who had been chosen for the leading roles, were exactly right for the parts. *Fuzz* was finally directed by Richard A. Colla and Burt Reynolds joined the cast.

De Palma decided to put Hollywood behind him, and shortly thereafter, he met producer Edward Pressman. Pressman had created a film company with Paul Williams (no relation to the composer) called Pressman-Williams. They wanted to offer an alternative to the Hollywood production by doing low budget films, comparable to *Easy Rider* (1969), that had commercial appeal. Paul Williams had successively directed *Out of It* (1970), starring Jon Voight, *The Revolutionary* (1970), and *Dealing* (1972); the three films had the same style and were all youth dramas. Having failed miserably at the box office, Pressman-Williams was in desperate need of a project and a director that would save them from bankruptcy. They were immediately thrilled by the idea of doing *Sisters* with De Palma. The picture was a horror thriller—though De Palma likes to refer to it as a suspense movie—that suited the producers' desire to change their image by switching genres. De Palma had co-written *Sisters* with Louisa Rose in 1970. His association with Pressman-Williams pleased him, since he realized that a return to independent production, without a studio or a distributor, would give him back his autonomy and his control over the film.

SISTERS *(Blood Sisters* in England) *(1973)*

SYNOPSIS: Danielle (Margot Kidder), a young, seductive model, meets Philip Woode (Lisle Wilson), a handsome black businessman, on a television game show called "Peeping Toms." They decide to spend the evening together, but in the middle of their dinner, they are interrupted by Emil Breton (William Finley), Danielle's ex-husband. Later, after they get rid of the obnoxious man, Philip spends the night at Danielle's, and he pays little attention to the large scar on the woman's right hip. The next morning, Philip is awakened by the sound of Danielle arguing with Dominique, her twin sister; today is their birthday, and Dominique is jealous of the presence of a stranger in the living room. Suddenly, Danielle doesn't feel well, and asks Philip to go to the drugstore to get her pills. On his way back, the young man buys a birthday cake, and when he presents it to Dominique, asleep on the couch, she grabs the knife and stabs him to death. Grace Collier (Jennifer Salt), a journalist, witnesses the murder from her window. She immediately calls the police, who seem reluctant to believe her; Grace is the author of a column on police brutality entitled "Why We Call Them Pigs!" Grace's argument with the detective (Dolph Sweet) of the local precinct leaves enough time for Emil Breton and Danielle to clean the apartment and hide the body of the victim in the folding couch. Of course, the police find no evidence of the crime. Grace hires Larch (Charles Durning), a private detective, to help her solve the mystery. Larch is determined to follow a moving van after he guesses that Philip's body was in the folding couch. Grace discovers that Danielle had once had a Siamese twin named Dominique, who died when they were separated by Doctor Emil Breton. Grace's investigations bring her to an asylum, where Emil keeps her prisoner. Emil hypnotizes Grace to erase Philip's murder from her memory. He then tries to exorcize Danielle's split personality complex—brought on by the fact that she could not accept her

Siamese sister's death and felt responsible for it. Danielle had been in love with Emil, and when she got pregnant, Dominique tried to kill her. Danielle lost her child and Emil separated the bond between the sisters, causing Dominique's death. Each time a man seduced Danielle, it reminded her of Emil, and Dominique's vengeful personality took over. Finally, Danielle becomes Dominique one last time and murders Emil. By killing him, she is at last liberated from her sister's personality. Grace is safe, but because of the hypnosis she cannot remember ever witnessing Philip's murder. As for Larch, the private detective, he is still following the couch on its journey across the Canadian border.

Sisters was a new step in De Palma's career. Rather than improvising, as he had done in his early films, De Palma realized that the genre of this picture demanded scrupulous preparation in order to be suspenseful. All the shots were designed on story boards, and De Palma's goal was to create a surreal atmosphere as well as to shock the audience with violent scenes. De Palma wanted, at all cost, to avoid making a gratuitous slasher picture, and felt that if he gave the film an unconventional look, it could stand out as an art film. De Palma wanted *Sisters* to appeal to an intellectual audience, just as Luis Buñuel's *Un Chien Andalou* (1928) had become a classic of surrealism despite the gruesomeness of the scene of a razor slashing an eyeball. Also, De Palma decided to play games with the audience and test his ability to manipulate filmgoers; he set up Margot Kidder as the sympathetic character, and hoped to have the audience identify with her until he revealed that she was in fact a psychotic killer.

With *Sisters*, De Palma explored the themes that he had already brought up in his previous films, and that recur throughout almost all of his work. *Sisters* dealt with voyeurism, sexuality, guilt, and the split personality all at once, and the interconnections between these themes—which will be explored in the chapters that follow—created a pattern that defined De Palma's obsession with human disturbances.

Sisters contained a great deal of black humor, which De Palma used for comic relief. For example, right after the murder of Philip Woode, while Emil Breton is cleaning up the apartment, he slips ridiculously on the floor before exiting the room. Later, Grace Collier also slips after she finds the birthday cake—proving that indeed, she has a twin sister named Dominique (the inscription on the cake reads "Happy Birthday Dominique and Danielle"—in Danielle's kitchen. Her fall to the floor destroys the evidence, as the cake smashes at the detective's feet.

Sisters was undoubtedly the first time De Palma worked with a screenplay that was consistent, and that had a lead and a strong structure supported by excellent characters. De Palma rehearsed with his cast for a month before the shooting began: William Finley played Doctor Emil Breton, Margot Kidder was the psychotic Siamese twin, Jennifer Salt, the journalist and witness to the murder, Mary Davenport, Salt's mother in the film (as well as in real life), and Charles Durning, Larch, the private detective. It was during the preparation period that De Palma decided to make changes in the screenplay. In the original script, it was not Emil Breton who cleaned up the apartment after the murder of Woode, but Danielle herself. She also hid the birthday cake in the refrigerator—behind a package of fresh calves' liver. The encounter between Larch and Grace Collier was more developed—Larch at first posed as a window cleaner to prove to Grace how efficiently he could work undercover. In the screenplay, Emil Breton knew that Larch was after the body that Danielle had hidden in a folding couch. Breton retrieved the body and hired movers to take the couch away, convinced that Larch would follow their truck to its destination. Breton and Danielle then cut up Woode's body into pieces with a large surgical saw and put them into two suitcases which they threw in the river. This scene was written as part of a flashback, but De Palma finally decided that Philip Woode's body should not leave the couch.

The screenplay was less clever than the film. For example, Danielle received from the "Peeping Toms" TV game show "a complete wardrobe of multicolored pantyhose from Marchioness, makers of fine lingerie," instead of the set of cutlery she received in the movie. The knives were, of course, more germane to the subject matter of the film, as Danielle later grabbed one to murder Philip Woode. Also, the screenplay called for more gory moments, including a shot of Emil Breton sawing off the bond of flesh between the Siamese sisters. In the end, De Palma settled for less blood-bath scenes, and the murders are more suggestive than graphic. De Palma's intention with *Sisters* was not to disgust his audience, but to shock them, by luring them into believing Dominique was still alive. Overdoing the murder scenes would have spoiled the surprising twist, and reduced its impact.

Brian De Palma wanted Bernard Herrmann, the composer famous for his work for Hitchcock, to write the score for *Sisters*. He knew that Herrmann was hard to get along with, but he was ready to accept his storminess for the sake of his film. During the scoring of *Torn Curtain* (1966), Herrmann's relationship with Hitchcock had totally deteriorated. Hitchcock was being pressured by Universal studio to get Herrmann to write a "commercial" score; the musician refused to be controlled by the studio, and since Hitchcock was not on his side either, he let the production hire John Addison to do the music for the film. Herrmann then moved to England where he lived a reclusive life.

De Palma was convinced that Herrmann's music would make *Sisters* scarier than it already was, based on the fact that his scores to Hitchcock's pictures had always added to the tension of the films. To give an idea of the kind of scoring he desired, De Palma put together a soundtrack for *Sisters* using music excerpts from the Hitchcock films *Marnie* (1964) for the love scenes, *Psycho* (1960) for the murder scenes, and *Vertigo* (1958) for the dream sequence. Herrmann had, of course, scored all three movies. When he heard De Palma's dummy soundtrack, he ordered him to stop the screening and said: "I don't want to hear *Marnie* when I'm looking at your movie. How can I think of anything new with that playing?" Suddenly, working with Herrmann reminded De Palma of dealing with Orson Welles during the shooting of *Get to Know Your Rabbit*. De Palma wrote, in the *Village Voice* in 1973:

> He, too, berated for what he considered bad judgment. But the difference between Herrmann and Welles was that Herrmann passionately cared that what was decided was right and threw his whole being into it; Welles knew just as well what was right—he had just given up fighting for it.

The only indication that Herrmann liked *Sisters* was the fact that he compared it to his memorable experience with Hitchcock on *Psycho*. Herrmann had succeeded in convincing Hitchcock to play his famous score for the shower scene, when originally the director had wanted the sequence to be silent. De Palma was pleased with the analogy, but he started a new fight with the composer when he announced that he wanted the opening credits to be short and free of any musical accompaniment. "No title music?" Herrmann said. "Nothing horrible happens in your picture for the first half hour. You need something to scare them right away. The way you do it, they'll walk out." De Palma argued by saying that the murder in *Psycho* didn't happen until forty minutes into the film. Herrmann got even more furious. "You are not Hitchcock!" he replied. "He can make his movies as slow as he wants in the beginning! And you know why?" De Palma shook his head "Because he is Hitchcock and they will wait! They know something terrible is going to happen and they'll wait until it does. They'll watch your movie for ten minutes and then they'll go home to their televisions!"

De Palma knew that Herrmann was right. It had been wrong for him to expect the composer to write for *Sisters* a score that he thought already existed. De Palma also realized that he had insulted Herrmann by underestimating his creativity to the point of giving him "samples" of the kind of music he wanted for his picture. And the director agreed with Herrmann that the opening credits should have music to set the genre and the mood of the movie.

Everything seemed to be working out between the two men when Herrmann announced that he would score the film using Moog synthesizers. De Palma, at this point, seriously questioned the composer's judgment. De Palma had thought all along that *Sisters* should have an imposing orchestrated soundtrack, and suddenly Herrmann was simplifying the concept with synthesizers. But surprisingly, De Palma didn't argue with Herrmann. Finally, when De Palma first heard the music with the film, he couldn't leave his seat, and he knew that it would have the same effect on the audience.

Ultimately, De Palma declared that working with Herrmann had been one of the highlights of his career. *Sisters* became a cult classic of the suspense/horror genre. The *Hollywood Reporter* called it "the most genuinely frightening film since Alfred Hitchcock's *Psycho*." The film was not a huge financial success when it was distributed by producer Samuel Z. Arkoff's American International Release, but those who saw the film could already see that De Palma had a fresh and welcome vision of the genre. *Sisters* won De Palma a "license to kill"—a privilege that he would use in most of his subsequent films, and with which he would become one of the most controversial contemporary directors.

PHANTOM OF THE PARADISE (1974)

SYNOPSIS: Swan (Paul Williams), the world's most powerful record producer, is about to open a new music club called the Paradise. He has stolen the unfinished rock opera written by Winslow Leach (William Finley), a young, naive, and unknown composer. Swan sets Leach up for an arrest on drug charges, and has him locked up in jail. Leach escapes, and while he plans the destruction of Swan's factory, his face is accidentally smashed by a record press. Disfigured and having lost his voice, Leach puts on a mask, and a cape and becomes the Phantom of the Paradise. Leach offers to complete his rock opera only if Swan swears to let Phoenix (Jessi-ca Harper), the woman he loves, perform his songs. The two men sign a contract marked in blood, but Swan doesn't keep his prom-ise; he hires Beef (Gerrit Graham), an effeminate singer, to perform the rock opera. Leach gets Beef electrocuted during the concert in front of a delirious audience. Finally, Phoenix successfully replaces Beef, and her singing is a triumph. Swan decides to marry Phoenix, and plans to murder her in public to create a "singular sensation." Winslow discovers that Swan is under a contract with the Devil that assures him everlasting youth and success. Leach burns the videotapes of both his own contract with Swan and the pact between the record producer and the Devil. Swan dies, and Leach subsequently meets with his own tragic end.

Immediately after *Sisters*, De Palma teamed with Pressman-Williams on another film—*Phantom of the Paradise*. De Palma had been wanting to make this film for five years. He had been seduced by the idea of a composer who, having had his opera ripped off, endeavors to kill the people who stole it, and put on the girl he loves to sing it the way he wants it to be sung. De Palma loved rock 'n' roll (and still does), and the concept of doing a contemporary version of *The Phantom of the Opera* set in a modern rock palace thrilled him.

Ed Pressman budgeted the film at $1.2 million. He took the project from one major studio to another—and ended up traveling from one broken promise to another. Tired of the game, De Palma brought *Phantom* to the attention of A&M Records where he met the composer, Paul Williams, who loved the project, and whose enthusiasm ultimately triggered its production.

Phantom of the Paradise was based on the classic novel, *The Phantom of the Opera* and on the legend of Faust. It was, however, more of a satire on the world of entertainment, and in part mirrored De Palma's frustration at being an artist at the mercy of big film studios.

At first, Paul Williams wanted to play the role of the Phantom. He had also had bad experiences at the juncture of big business and art. Like De Palma, he identified with the manipulated character and thought he had found, by playing the part, a rather cynical way to get back at those who had used him in the music industry. Ironically, Williams was finally cast to play the evil Swan; William Finley got the part of Phantom, Gerrit Graham played the eccentric Beef, and Jessica Harper, for whom it was a feature debut, was cast as Phoenix, chosen over many other actresses/singers including Sissy Spacek (who reportedly didn't sing all that well!). Instead, Spacek got a credit as set decorator, along with her husband, Jack Fisk—who would later design the production of *Carrie* (1976) and direct his wife in *Raggedy Man* (1981) and *Violets Are Blue* (1986).

As with *Sisters*, all the scenes had been designed, prepared, and rehearsed long in advance. *Phantom of the Paradise* confirmed that De Palma had developed his artistic awareness. His visual style both in *Sisters* and in *Phantom* expressed the subconscious in images, showing that De Palma was trying to impose his creative self. Some scenes, such as Beef's concert, were highly stylized—the set on stage was a tribute to Robert Wiene's *Cabinet of Doctor Caligari* (1919), and Beef's number was a reference to the classic *Frankenstein* (1931). These were juxtaposed with sequences like the wedding of Swan and Phoenix, which had the feel of a live news report.

Phantom of the Paradise was built around a structure that has today become the style of music videos. Some songs in the film, like the one during which the Phantom finishes his opera, were expressed through a montage of images without order or coherence, as in a dream.

Despite the long period of preparation, problems started almost immediately after the first days of shooting. The scenes took too much time to set up and the film quickly fell behind schedule. Because of this, De Palma was able to shoot only eighty percent of what he had planned to film. The main segment that was never shot was the last scene—it was the burial of Beef, which featured all the characters singing one last cantata. The scene was replaced by an assemblage of the best moments in the film, which evidently had a lesser effect than what had originally been planned—though again it created a structure that would later become the distinctive style of music videos.

But the problems didn't stop there. De Palma was sued by Universal Pictures, who owned the rights to *The Phantom of the Opera*. They thought De Palma had done a remake of their film, and wanted him to pay for the rights to use the story. De Palma ultimately settled the case. (Ironically, the original title of the film was *Phantom*, which was also the name of a comic book super hero. In order to avoid any lawsuit from that source, De Palma had been forced to change his title to *Phantom of the Paradise*.) But the biggest problem to settle came when Atlantic, a record company, told De Palma he couldn't use the label Swan Song Enterprises in his film because they had a subsidiary named Swan Song Records. The film was already completed and the logo appeared in many key scenes. De Palma had to change the label directly on the print, through a photographic mat effect, to Death Records.

But in the end, because of all these problems, everyone had heard of the film, and De Palma and Pressman received six distributor offers. They accepted the $2 million deal proposed by Twentieth Century Fox. *Greetings, Hi, Mom!*, and *Sisters* had been distributed by small releasing companies. As a consequence, the films could not face the competition from the big studios—whose pictures had priority in the best theaters—and were booked for a limited amount of weeks in theaters of lesser importance. Warner had released *Get to Know Your Rabbit* to fulfill their contract with the producer of the film. De Palma, Pressman, and Williams were confident that Fox would assure *Phantom* a wide release. Unfortunately, the studio had bigger, more glamorous pictures to put their money into and—also considering that the press on *Phantom* was not encouraging—Fox decided not to waste their energy on pushing the film to exhibitors. Vincent Canby wrote in *The New York Times*:

> Mr. De Palma is a very funny man, as he has shown in marvelously eccentric comedies such as *Greetings* and *Hi, Mom!*, and even in his more conventional films, *Get to Know Your Rabbit* and *Sisters*. Compared with even the least of these, *Phantom of the Paradise* is an elaborate disaster, full of the kind of facetious humor you might find on bumper stickers and cocktail coasters.

The criticism was hardly justified. A year later, *The Rocky Horror Picture Show*, also distributed by Fox, would receive equally unjustified rave reviews; *Rocky* had more "facetious humor" than the De Palma film. Again, because of its lack of exposure, *Phantom of the Paradise* was not a financial success, nor did it win critical acclaim. However, the film became an instant cult classic in Europe, and received the Grand Prize at the Avoriaz horror film festival in France. Since its release in 1974, *Phantom of the Paradise* has consistently played in art movie houses in Europe. It is rarely shown in the U.S.

OBSESSION (1976)

> SYNOPSIS: Michael Courtland (Cliff Robertson) is a successful busi-
> nessman. He lives happily in New Orleans with Elizabeth
> (Genevieve Bujold), his wife, and Amy, his daughter. Michael's
> family is kidnapped, and the blackmail attempt ends tragically when
> he fails to bring the ransom—Elizabeth and Amy die in a car
> accident during a chase with the police. Years later, Michael goes

to Italy on a business trip with La Salle (John Lithgow), his partner. He visits the church where he had first met Elizabeth and he talks to Sandra, a young woman who is his wife's exact look-alike. They fall in love and go back to Louisiana to get married. However, Michael's psychiatrist, friends, and partners try to discourage his wedding plans; they know that Michael is infatuated with Sandra only because she reminds him so much of Elizabeth. One morning, Michael realizes that Sandra has been kidnapped under the same circumstances as his wife and daughter years ago. Michael begs La Salle to loan him money to pay the ransom, but the partner treacherously substitutes paper for the bank notes. Surprisingly, it's Sandra herself who comes to get the ransom—she is in fact Amy, Michael's daughter. Amy had not died in the car accident. Convinced that her father hated his family, she had accepted an offer to team up with La Salle to blackmail and ruin Michael. Michael discovers La Salle's evil schemes, kills him, takes the money, and is determined to shoot Amy, whom he believes is still only his wife's look-alike. After trying to kill herself, Amy sees her father and runs into his arms. Michael suddenly understands that he is holding his daughter, and all is forgiven.

Obsession was written by Brian De Palma and Paul Schrader (the screenwriter of Martin Scorsese's *Taxi Driver* [1976], and the director of *Hardcore* [1979], *American Gigolo* [1980], *Cat People* [1982], and *Mishima* [1985]), based on a story by Brian De Palma. *Obsession* was originally titled *Double Ransom* and then *Deja-Vu*. It took George Litto, the producer of the film, two years to assemble the budget. Since the film was again an independent production, De Palma received the right to have total control over the picture—but the director encountered the same problems he had faced during *Phantom of the Paradise*, and was unable to shoot all of the scenes he had written. Vilmos Zsigmond, the famous director of photography, was a real perfectionist, and his own obsession with details, combined with the intricate shots De Palma's directing required, put the production behind schedule. Bernard Herrmann was brought in on *Obsession* during the early stages of production, and he had a consequent influence over the structure of the movie. Herrmann's score for the film remained his favorite until his death.

Herrmann convinced De Palma to make drastic changes in the end of the movie, which had dissatisfied the director himself. The final chapter of *Obsession*, they felt, was unbelievable and absurd. Paul Schrader, who had come up with the ending, felt insulted and betrayed by De Palma and Herrmann. In Schrader's script, *Obsession* didn't end at the airport. Cliff Robertson was arrested and locked up in an asylum. Fifteen years later, free at last, he returned to Florence with the intention of killing his daughter. He found her in the same church where he had met his wife in the past, and Robertson realized that his daughter had lost her memory. She was subjected to a session of hypnosis during which she remembered the events of her life and understood that her father had never been responsible for her mother's death. Daughter and father mutually forgave each other. This segment was totally abandoned. *Obsession* simply ends with Robertson embracing Bujold. Needless to say, from then on the working relationship between De Palma and Schrader disintegrated. The arguments about the screenplay, which occurred during the filming, also inevitably slowed down the schedule. De Palma told the French magazine *Les cahiers du cinéma* that Schrader had talent but that his stories suffered from structural problems. According to De Palma, Schrader often got carried away, and his plots had a lack of substance and logic.

The mood of *Obsession* was quite unusual. The pacing was purposely slow, but it killed the film's commercial appeal when Litto shopped for a distributor. The movie didn't see daylight for eight months after its completion. Finally, a deal came through with Columbia Pictures and *Obsession* was released—only one month before *Carrie*. The reviews acknowledged the originality of De Palma's visual style—for example, his idea of having Genevieve Bujold play herself as a little girl in a flashback scene was remarkable and innovative. (De Palma actually tried to reiterate this concept in *Carrie* but the sequence didn't fit the film as well as it had in *Obsession*, and was abandoned.)

"An immensely important cinematic work with a throbbing, lusty score by Bernard Herrmann . . . like Hitchcock at the top of his form," wrote Rex Reed in the *New York Daily News*. ". . . eerie and haunting . . . Unforgettable," commented Liz Smith in *Cosmopolitan*. Herrmann's score got reviews almost unparalleled by any other film music composer: "Herrmann's music, beautifully recorded in London, is among his last and his best as well; it would make blank film compelling," wrote *Variety*. "It's a magnificent, haunting score that, on first hearing, seems to rank with this composer's finest work," said the *Hollywood Reporter*.

But *Obsession* was still a tough film to market: it was like Hitchcock, but it wasn't Hitchcock! The connection made between De Palma and the master of suspense didn't work in favor of the film. *Obsession* grossed a modest $4.468 million at the box office. It was evident that De Palma was respected in the film industry, since, despite the fact that none of his films—except perhaps *Greetings*—had yet been a huge financial hit, he kept getting offers.

The problem with the film was that it had no humor in it; it was a very dark romantic story that suggested incestuous feelings between a daughter and her father. Still, *Obsession* worked as a suspense film, as well as an unconventional drama and love story. Maybe De Palma should have gone even further in elaborating a more complex relationship between the father and his daughter. Maybe the problem with *Obsession* was that it wasn't shocking enough. . . .

CARRIE (1976)

SYNOPSIS: Carrie White (Sissy Spacek) is a total stranger to life. An outcast in her small town high school, she lives with an oppressive evangelist mother (Piper Laurie). But Carrie discovers that she has telekinetic powers. One day, Carrie gets her first period in front of her classmates in the showers of the gym locker rooms. She is frightened by the sight of the blood running between her legs, and all the other girls humiliate her. Sue Snell (Amy Irving), one of Carrie's classmates, feels guilty about laughing at the poor girl in the showers and asks Tommy Ross (William Katt), her gorgeous boyfriend, to take Carrie to the prom. Tommy hesitates, but finally agrees. Chris Hargenson (Nancy Allen), Carrie's worst enemy, has been refused her prom ticket by Miss Collins (Betty Buckley), the gym teacher, because of Chris's bad attitude. With the complicity of her dumb date, Billy Nolan (John Travolta), Chris plans to humiliate Carrie by dropping a bucket filled with pig's blood on her at the prom. Carrie goes with Tommy to the prom despite her mother's warnings. Carrie and Tommy begin to fall in love and are elected—as planned by Chris—Queen and King of the prom. Then, fatally, Carrie is covered with the blood and the bucket hits Tommy, killing him instantly. Carrie transforms the prom into a circus of death with her telekinetic powers. Back home, she is confronted by her mother, who tries to kill her "sinful" daughter; Carrie responds with her supernatural forces and neutralizes the madwoman. Ultimately, the powers of Evil make the house collapse and both Carrie and Mrs. White are engulfed, with it, into the ground. For Sue Snell, the only one from her school to have survived the holocaust, the memory of Carrie will always haunt her dreams.

It was a girl by the name of Carrie who suddenly brought an incredible breakthrough to De Palma's career. A writer friend of Brian De Palma had told him about a book entitled *Carrie*, written by a then-unknown novelist named Stephen King. At the time, De Palma had received an offer to do the screen adaptation of Mary Higgins Clark's *Where Are The Children?* which luckily he never made. Immediately after he had read *Carrie*, De Palma contacted Paul Monash, the producer who held the film rights to the novel. He found out that Monash had already called George Litto to submit the project to De Palma. The screenplay was written by Lawrence D. Cohen, who would later write the film adaptation of Peter Straub's bestseller *Ghost Story* (1981). De Palma immediately went into pre-production with a $1.6 million budget; *Carrie* was shot in fifty days for $1.8 million.

Throughout his career, Brian De Palma has launched the careers of many actors, including Robert De Niro and Jill Clayburgh. *Carrie* brought attention to Sissy Spacek, John Travolta, Nancy Allen (who would become Mrs. De Palma in 1980 and divorce the director three years later), Amy Irving (today married to Steven Spielberg), Betty Buckley (one of Broadway's finest stars), William Katt, and P.J. Soles (the ex–Mrs. Dennis Quaid). The supporting cast included Priscilla Pointer, Irving's mother in the film and in life.

De Palma directed his auditions for *Carrie*, coincidentally, with George Lucas, who was casting *Star Wars* (1977). Carrie Fisher met De Palma for the role of Carrie and ended up playing Princess Leia in Lucas's space saga. Lucas, on his side, had seen both William Katt and Amy Irving for his film, but they instead landed roles in De Palma's tale of the supernatural. When Sissy Spacek auditioned, De Palma wanted her for the part of Chris, Carrie's worst enemy. Finally, when she showed up dressed as miserably as Carrie in the story, Spacek was so convincing that De Palma immediately changed his mind. It was Nancy Allen who received the honor of pulling the rope attached to the bucket of blood. Ten years later, Allen recalled:

> It's strange, but the first scene in *Carrie* takes place in the showers of a locker room, and I heard of the film for the first time when I was stepping out of the steam room at my gym, and bumped into the casting director of *Carrie*! In the film, I got to play Chris, a real bitch. I loved it because underneath it all, I think that Chris is just misunderstood. The shooting was very difficult, especially for the shower scene because we all had to be naked. [Amy Irving is the only actress who is not naked in the scene.] We even had to sign some releases because some of the girls didn't want to do it and the producer was afraid they might walk off the set. But

Brian was so wonderful that he gave us a lot of confidence and we understood that after all, this was no big deal!

De Palma spent a great deal of time rehearsing with the actors. William Katt commented:

We had solved all the problems before we got on the film, and once we got on the actual time when we were shooting, Brian worked more with the camera. He allowed us a lot of freedom because he knew exactly what we were capable of. He trusted us and it allowed him to be more focused on the visual part of the movie.

Piper Laurie hadn't been in a film for several years, but she had heard about the project through her neighbor who worked for United Artists. Laurie arrived for her audition dressed for the part and when De Palma saw her, he instinctively knew that she was Carrie's mother.

During the casting, De Palma was working on reshaping the screenplay. *Carrie* was the first novel by Stephen King to be adapted to the screen. Though the translation of his books to films often had less impact than his writing, King liked De Palma's *Carrie*. There were, however, many changes made in translating the book onto film. The novel was structured like a flashback, and the story was told by the character played by Amy Irving in the film. De Palma added to the picture a greater shock value—in the book, Carrie's mother didn't die impaled by kitchen cutlery, but of a heart attack provoked by her daughter's powers.

With *Carrie*, De Palma was confronted for the first time with sophisticated mechanical effects. He called on Gregory M. Auer, who had already worked on *Phantom of the Paradise*, to orchestrate Carrie's supernatural forces. The most challenging scene was the death of Piper Laurie, stabbed by knives flying into her body; the cutlery was in fact placed on transparent strings that were attached to the actress's bathrobe.

Auer also worked closely with Jack Fisk on the apocalyptic destruction of Carrie's house. Originally, rocks were supposed to collapse on a small scale house, but the results were not convincing; Fisk finally decided to simply burn down Carrie's home. Brian De Palma declared on the set of the film: "Special effects are like blind faith—you have to tell your man what you want to do, and hope to God when you get there he's figured out how to do it." But the technical challenge obviously didn't worry De Palma all that much, considering that his next project, *The Fury*, got him even more involved with special mechanical and make-up effects.

Naturally, De Palma would have wanted Bernard Herrmann to write the score for *Carrie*, but the composer had died shortly before. De Palma chose to collaborate for the first time with Italian composer Pino Donaggio; Donaggio went on to write the brilliant soundtracks to De Palma's *Home Movies, Dressed to Kill, Blow Out,* and *Body Double.* To pay tribute to Herrmann—and also to have the final word over the composer who had humiliated him when he had used the Hitchcock scores as examples of what he wanted for *Sisters*—De Palma employed the shrieking sound of violins, which Herrmann had composed for the shower scene in *Psycho,* several times to accompany Carrie's use of her powers.

Carrie grossed fifteen times what it had cost. Still, De Palma was not satisfied with the way United Artists had handled the release of his picture. De Palma had wished that *Carrie* would become a phenomenon, and inspire attention comparable to the controversy *The Exorcist* (1973) had created. For De Palma, *Carrie* was a serious movie, and he wanted mature audiences to see it—not only horror fans (and guys waiting for their dates to jump from their seats onto their laps!) United Artists released *Carrie* for Halloween, and marketed it as a popcorn movie.

Stephen King admitted that the film had more style than his novel. He said that the nightmare sequence at the end had totally surprised him. King recalled:

> The first time I saw *Carrie* with an audience was at a preview a week and a half before Halloween. The audience was full of black people. I thought: they are going to rate the hell out of this picture. What are they going to think about a skinny little white girl with her menstrual problems? And that's the way it started, and then, little by little, they got on her side, you know, and when she started doing her shtick, I mean, they're going, tear it up!—Go for it!—and all this other stuff. I knew it was going to be a hit!

Brian De Palma had created for *Carrie* an innovative style which became a classic example of the horror genre. *Carrie* was a horror film with feelings; it also had a dramatic ending, and was a statement on how being "different" in our society can eventually become a nightmare. Carrie was human and easy to identify with. The variety of De Palma's visual elements confirmed that he had a film language all his own, as well as extraordinary technical skill. The prom scene, for example, required six weeks of editing, during which De Palma assembled 150 shots into a highly stylized buildup.

Sissy Spacek and Piper Laurie were both nominated for Academy Awards. Spacek lost the Best Actress award to Faye Dunaway, who received the Oscar for *Network*, and Beatrice Straight was chosen over Laurie as Best Supporting Actress for her role in *Network*. After its Oscar nominations, *Carrie* received a little more recognition as an important film than it had at its opening. *Carrie* was more than a commercial success. It was a critical success: "*Carrie* really delivers its punch," wrote Frank Rich in the *New York Post*, "and it does so with style, wit and feeling. The film is full of real people, who are brought to life by an extraordinarily sensitive cast, and its camera movement is galvanized by the director's brooding compassion." On the other hand, Rex Reed, for example, found *Carrie*, "obscene, pretentious, dopey, violent, and unintentionally hilarious." (His words might as well be used to describe his own review of the film.)

Brian De Palma recalls feeling frustrated when comparing the grosses of *Carrie* to Steven Spielberg's *Jaws* (1975). *Carrie* had been an enormous hit and had given De Palma worldwide fame, but it was nothing in comparison to the colossal success of *Jaws*. He was hoping that with his next film, *The Fury*, his name would climb up there, next to George Lucas and Steven Spielberg's—and maybe, who knows, soon surpass them. . . .

THE FURY (1978)

SYNOPSIS: Robin (Andrew Stevens) is a young man with telekinetic powers. He is kidnapped by Childress (John Cassavetes), an agent whose mission is to use Robin's abilities for political blackmail. Peter (Kirk Douglas), Robin's father, wants to save his son—who believes him dead—and decides to eliminate Childress. Peter is helped by Hester (Carrie Snodgress), his mistress, who spies for him at the cost of her own life. Before her death, Hester had discovered that Robin has a "psychic twin," a girl of the same age with identical powers named Gillian (Amy Irving). Gillian is able to locate Robin. In the meantime, the young man has gone out of control as a result of the tests Childress has put him through. Robin becomes evil and refuses to recognize his father when he is confronted by him. Robin dies, and Peter kills himself from despair. Childress is ready to start all over with Gillian, Robin's legitimate replacement. But Gillian only fakes her willingness to cooperate, and with her powers, she leads Childress to an explosive end.

The Fury, De Palma's next film, was based on a novel by John Farris. Farris wrote the screenplay for producer Frank Yablans, of *Silver Streak* (1976) and *The Other Side of Midnight* (1977) fame. With *The Fury*, De Palma wanted to do what he had done already with *Carrie*, but on a larger scale. The director's intention was also to prove that you didn't necessarily have to be a Hollywood-based director to make a blockbuster hit. Yablans had known De Palma from the time he had helped finance *Greetings* and *Hi, Mom!* and had been impressed by the filmmaker's rise in the industry. Yablans wanted *The Fury* to be one of the most spectacular films ever made, and he invested in an all-star cast to help him attain his goal. Kirk Douglas, John Cassavetes, Carrie Snodgress, Amy Irving, Andrew Stevens, Fiona Lewis, and Carol Rossen played the leading roles, and were supported by the usual De Palma crowd, which included Charles Durning, William Finley, and Rutanya Alda. Daryl Hannah had a small part as one of Irving's classmates, as did Melodie Thomas, who had played the role of Tippi Hedren as a little girl in Alfred Hitchcock's *Marnie*.

Brian De Palma was working with his biggest cast and largest budget yet ($5.5 million). Throughout the shooting, the director realized that the story had too many characters and, feeling that the plot was too complicated, he asked John Farris to simplify the story. Minor characters like William Finley's appeared in fewer scenes, and De Palma cut out a sequence during which Andrew Stevens rapes Fiona Lewis, as well as a shot of Kirk Douglas "giving the finger" to John Cassavetes before he dies. These changes gave the film a more comprehensive autonomy, and also limited the characters to lesser dimensions.

The Fury involved a lot of special effects. William Tuttle and Rick Baker created replicas of the bodies of John Cassavetes and Fiona Lewis. Dick Smith made an uncredited contribution to the film by creating the effects for the blood and for the pulsing vein on Andrew Stevens's forehead. A. D. Flowers worked on the mechanical effects for the scenes of levitation. The two most complicated scenes were the disruption of a Ferris wheel and the explosion of John Cassavetes. Stevens is in an amusement park when he suddenly sees a group of Arabs climbing onto a Ferris wheel; it reminds him that his father has supposedly been killed by Arabs, and with his powers, he provokes an accident. (Yablans found this concept racist and would have rather had Stevens use his evil forces against a girl who refuses his advances.) The final scene originally showed Amy Irving forcing John Cassavetes to drown in his own blood in his bathtub. Instead, De Palma took on the challenging task of making Cassavetes explode; the scene was shot with ten cameras that covered all the possible angles on a mannequin loaded with explosives.

But the most spectacular scene in *The Fury* is Amy Irving's escape from Cassavetes' Paragon Institute. The sequence was shot partly in slow motion, and John Williams' brilliant score, combined with De Palma's skill at building up the unbearable suspense of this climactic moment, make it the best scene in the film. The sequence required six days of shooting in the streets of Chicago.

Frank Yablans was very active on the set of his film. He directed the scene during which Kirk Douglas jumps from a building onto train tracks, and he appeared as an extra who is killed during Irving's escape.

The Fury was not well received by the critics. The film was described as "silly," and as "an all-time bummer," and Rex Reed advised: "See *The Fury* only if you hate yourself!" The truth is that *The Fury* is probably one of De Palma's best films. The filming is exquisite, and it is no more confusing than, for example, Hitchcock's *North by Northwest* (1959). The problem with *The Fury* was that it was different from *Carrie*, and critics and audiences expected to be served "the same meal" they had enjoyed with De Palma's previous film. As a result, word of mouth on the film was poor, and it grossed a modest $11.1 million at the box office.

To many, *The Fury* was also too gory and too graphic. The U.S. Catholic Conference condemned the film as "an affront to human dignity"—the citation meant that the Conference regarded the picture as morally objectionable for American Roman Catholics. The Conference was particularly upset about the use of "an aging couple trapped in a crime-ridden environment and obliged to care for a disabled mother as comic relief." In a review in the April 1978 issue of *Film and Broadcasting, The Fury* was rapped for "violence, its unremitting depiction of bloodshed and its affront to human dignity." The controversy didn't work in De Palma's favor this time, and *The Fury* quickly disappeared from the screens.

Brian De Palma began to work on another project with Yablans entitled *The Demolished Man*, based on a science fiction thriller by Alfred Bester. *The Demolished Man* was an ambitious undertaking that never came to fruition partly because of the low financial returns of *The Fury*.

The Demolished Man takes place in the twenty-fourth century. It is the story of the powerful Ben Reich, who decides to murder his competitor, D'Courtney, after he refuses an association between their two industrial empires. Reich discovers at the end that D'Courtney had in fact accepted the deal, but that Reich had subconsciously convinced himself of the contrary; D'Courtney was actually his father, who had abandoned him when he was a child. The reasons why Reich had been deserted are explained by an expert in criminology:

> It was a closely guarded family secret. Reich was conceived and raised as nothing more than a business ploy to get around the interplanetary merger regulations. D'Courtney knew he couldn't merge his separate planetary conglomerates legally. So he created a pseudo-rival run by his own son. And Reich hated him for it.

Then the expert in criminology reveals that Reich suffers an emotional dysfunction. He had two personalities constantly in conflict; one side of him is normal, and the other side inhabited his subconscious, trying to force the conscious side to murder D'Courtney:

> Reich murdered his father. He discharged his hatred. But his super ego . . . his conscience, could not let him go unpunished for such a horrible crime. The conscious mind cannot face the conflict between the external world and its own unconscious.

The Demolished Man was a futuristic version of *Sisters* and *Dressed to Kill*. Characters in both those films also suffer from an inner duality and possess a subconscious personality which forces them to commit murderous acts. De Palma's script even envisioned a cure for the split personality syndrome. A detective explains:

> Reich has been administrated a new drug which will make the catatonic wish to escape come true. It disassociates the mind from the lower levels, sends it back to the womb, and lets it pretend it's being born to a new life all over again. He'll go through infancy, childhood, adolescence, and maturity in about five weeks.

Ben's internal conflict comes up in his dreams when a man with no face tries to murder him. The killer is, in fact, his true self trying to come out. The society of the twenty-fourth century according to De Palma has people with the ability to read another's mind without him knowing it. The ones with such talent were called "the peepers." Being able to read someone's thoughts was the voyeurism of the future; evidently, even in science fiction, De Palma was persistent in exploring this theme.

In the script, in order to kill D'Courtney and to have an alibi, Ben Reich arranges for the guests at a party to play Sardine, the game that had traumatized De Palma as a boy. Reich explains:

> One player is selected to be It. All the lights are turned out and the It hides anywhere in the house. After a few minutes, the players go to find the It, hunting separately. The first one who finds him does not reveal the fact but hides with him wherever he may be. Successively each player finding the Sardines joins them until all are hidden in one place and the last player, who is the loser, is left to wander alone in the dark.

There was an additional catch: all the players had to be naked. The loser was to be exposed to the assembly and become the victim of collective voyeurism.

De Palma had planned to have many scenes split in three images, essentially for the mind-peeping sessions. The peeper would be seen on the left, the thoughts of his victim in the middle, and the victim himself on the right side of the screen. *The Demolished Man* also had a *Star Wars* quality to it, with many space sequences . . . and creatures with six legs!

But because of the disappointment *The Fury* had caused the director, the producer, and Twentieth Century Fox (the distributor), *The Demolished Man* was put aside, and De Palma abandoned it as he got involved with projects that were, it seems, right up his alley.

THREE

HOME MOVIES *(1980)*

SYNOPSIS: Young Dennis Byrd (Keith Gordon) has decided to become the star of his own life. Until now, he's let himself be dominated by James (Gerrit Graham), his older brother, and neglected by his mother (Mary Davenport), who only has eyes for James, and by his father (Vincent Gardenia), a doctor specializing in the female anatomy. Motivated by the encouragements of The Maestro (Kirk Douglas), his mentor, Dennis starts to film his own existence. But he makes the mistake of falling in love with Kristina (Nancy Allen), his brother's fiancée. Kristina is an ex-prostitute who is ruled by Bunny, a stuffed rabbit she believes is real. To be certain that Kristina is ready to commit herself to a stable life, James puts her through a series of tests. But Kristina's true personality is revealed and she is banned from the family. Dennis finds himself alone again, on his way to college. At the train station, he bumps into Kristina, who is free at last from Bunny. Together, they decide to leave their problems behind them to head toward a life of culture, leisure, and . . . love.

During the editing of *The Fury*, De Palma called his old friend Wilford Leach at Sarah Lawrence College. De Palma was supposed to teach a class on independent filmmaking and thought it would be a good idea if the students could practice what they had been taught by making a low budget film that he would supervise. De Palma remembered that Terrence Malick (the director of *Days of Heaven* [1978]) had once said that he had been motivated to do independent films after he had seen *Greetings*. De Palma hoped that with *Home Movies*, he would encourage film students to pursue their careers in the film industry.

Steven Spielberg and George Lucas (they never visited the set) invested in the film. De Palma produced it for $400,000 and shared credit with Jack Temchin and Gil Adler. No one from the cast or crew was on salary, but every one had points on the gross of the movie. When Kirk Douglas was chosen to play the role of the Maestro, De Palma decided to take a director's credit; he feared that the film students might be intimidated by the fact that they were dealing with a movie star, and that their apprehension would jeopardize the quality of the picture. De Palma hired professionals at the head of each department.

Nancy Allen, Gerrit Graham, Keith Gordon, Mary Davenport, and Vincent Gardenia joined Douglas in this challenging project. Members of the cast and crew worked from twelve to eighteen hours a day, six days a week, for almost two months. Some scenes were technically sophisticated and one of them, a six-minute sequence with many angles filmed in one shot, required twenty-eight takes to get it right!

Working with Brian De Palma on the production of *Home Movies* was a unique opportunity for the students to get a feeling of what filmmaking was all about—to actually put their ambitions into practice. There were, of course problems, because not all of the students were trusted in their tasks, but overall the experience was a challenge unique in film history. Film student Rachel Feldman declared:

> Working on the set made me excited about film again. I've always loved movies, and from the time I was a kid, I wanted to act and now I want to direct films, but NYU grad film school depressed me. By the end of last year I was ready to say, okay, this is not working—I guess film is not for me. But by being on the set I remembered that film school is not film. It doesn't feel like the real thing—and I got excited again. I was thinking and observing and making movies in my head. I began reading and writing and seeing films again.

Karen D'Arc, another student, commented:

Home Movies was the crash course to end all crash courses. I've never worked harder and learned more in any seven-week period in my life. At first, I felt intimidated by the professional crew members and didn't want to disturb them to let me look through the camera, but right away in the first week, Brian made me assert myself. I was cleaning the side windows of a phone booth that was being shot head on. Brian said: "Karen, what is the camera going to see?" and I felt pretty silly. Then, Brian said that I shouldn't feel reluctant to tell the cameraman that I need to look through the camera before each shot.

On the other hand, student Laurie Newbound felt less enthusiastic about the whole experience:

The most frustrating aspect of making this film was the consistently inconsistent way in which the students were treated by the three executive producers. In the same hour we were treated as fully responsible professionals and conversely as children who rated no respect whatsoever. I would work days and days assembling, typing, editing, and mailing out contracts; a contract problem would come up and it would be kept from me. This kind of thing went on all the time in every area of production. This kind of secrecy made some students suspicious of the entire project and was wearing out student morale in general.

But these negative points were counterbalanced by the lesson the students could draw from them for the future. Gregg Horowitz summed up this lesson:

One of the most important things I learned during this project was thoroughly intangible, but so important precisely because it was intangible. When any group of people get together to work on a film, their egos will inevitably come into conflict. If the film is to be made smoothly, these conflicts have to be bound and gagged for the duration of the shoot. The mind of the director must be free to deal with the problems of the film, so he must have the ability to deal with conflicts in a manner not disruptive to his thought process, or else have someone—a producer, assistant director, et cetera—who can do it for him.

His experience on *Home Movies* allowed De Palma to define his view of film schools:

The real trouble with film school is that the people teaching are so far out of the industry that they don't give the students an idea of what's happening. Students should be exposed to the best people in the profession. If you study surgery, you study with the best doctors working in the hospital. You don't study with the ones who couldn't get the job.

When looking for a distributor for *Home Movies*, De Palma decided to refuse the deal offered by New Line Cinema, which wanted to buy the film for $250,000. On the other hand, United Artists Classics was proposing to pick up the film with no money up front, but offered higher points on the profits. De Palma went along with UA Classics because the company had a prestigious reputation and had distributed mainly quality products that received attention from the critics. Unfortunately, UA Classics didn't live up to its advance billing, mainly because the company worked with a very low publicity budget. *Home Movies* was released without proper advertising. De Palma himself ended up paying for ads in the newspapers. Critic Judy Stone acknowledged De Palma's efforts:

> It's a welcome relief to see a successful director who still has the ability to laugh at himself and the idiocies of an industry which is prepared to invest $40-odd million on overblown lemons, but doesn't have the vaguest notion of what to do about an offbeat joke on itself.

But most of the critics were negative, and *Home Movies* was dismissed as "a dismal, amateurish comedy" by Gene Siskel in the *Chicago Tribune*, and as "a disastrously unfunny movie" by Kevin Thomas in the *Los Angeles Times*.

Brian De Palma felt very bitter about his experience on *Home Movies*, and about the way it had been handled by its distributor:

> I spent two years of my life trying to teach a lesson and make this film, and I took a tremendous amount of risks making the movie. I dearly wanted it to be a success. And I wanted to reach people in the industry and tell them to take some time and look at a new generation of filmmakers, but we were ignored. Nobody cared. I was appalled. My attitude is that United Artists Classics totally blew my and my investors' money!

Nathaniel Kwit, then the Vice President of UA Classics, disagreed with that charge, and said that the film simply didn't appeal to enough people to deserve a wider release and a higher budget on advertising.

De Palma remained in contact with some of the students he had worked with on *Home Movies*. He later got a creative consultant credit on *The First*

Time (1982), a comedy directed by Charles Lowenthal and produced by Sam Irvin. Lowenthal had co-written *Home Movies*, and had a small part in the film, and Irvin had associate produced *Home Movies*.

Home Movies was an amusing and offbeat film, reminiscent of De Palma's early movies. It had the ambition and the format of *The Wedding Party*. Despite the confusion between the director and his distributor, *Home Movies* was a decent product. It was almost as if, after failing with *The Fury*, De Palma had decided to begin his career all over again, starting with a modest student picture, and gradually working his way to an ambitious, expensive film. . . .

DRESSED TO KILL (1980)

SYNOPSIS: Kate Miller (Angie Dickinson) is a middle-aged, sexually frustrated housewife. She complains to her psychiatrist, Dr. Robert Elliott (Michael Caine), about her second husband's pathetic performances in bed, and tests her sexual worth by trying to seduce him. Elliott turns down the proposition. Kate then picks up a handsome stranger (Ken Baker) in a museum and lives her wildest fantasies with him, first in a cab and then at his apartment. Before she leaves her one-afternoon stand, Kate finds papers that certify that the man has a venereal disease. Shattered, Kate rushes into the elevator, but has to back up after she realizes she's forgotten her wedding ring. When the elevator opens, Kate is slashed to death by a blond woman wearing dark glasses. Liz Blake (Nancy Allen), a "Park Avenue whore," is the only witness to the murder, and she becomes at once the star suspect and the murderess's next prey. Liz is saved from being killed by Peter (Keith Gordon), Kate's son, who is determined to unmask the killer, since the detective in charge of the case (Dennis Franz) is being totally uncooperative. Peter discovers that the murderess is one of Dr. Elliott's patients. Liz decides to seduce the shrink in order to check out the names in his appointment book. Liz arouses Elliott, and discovers that *he* was Bobbi, the murderess. Liz is saved by a female undercover cop (Susanna Clemm) hired by the sleazy detective who was, after all, on her side. It is revealed that Elliott was a transsexual with a split personality syndrome. He was about to make the final step toward a sex change operation, but his male side would not let him do it. Each time he was aroused by a woman, Bobbi—his female alter-ego—took over and killed the seductress. Elliott is locked up, but Bobbi still comes out to haunt Liz's nights.

De Palma cherished a project entitled *Prince of the City*, based on a book by Robert Dailey (the author of *Year of the Dragon*, which would be directed by Michael Cimino in 1985). Brian De Palma wanted to do the film with Robert De Niro. Orion Pictures owned the rights to *Prince*, and its executives began to grow impatient when De Niro announced that he wouldn't be available for a year. De Palma feared he would lose the project to another director, and suggested to Orion that he do a thriller called *Dressed to Kill* while waiting for De Niro. De Palma's agent at the time was Sue Mengers, who also represented Sidney Lumet. Lumet found out about *Prince of the City*, decided to offer his services to Orion Pictures, and got the job. De Palma changed agents and took *Dressed to Kill* to Filmways Pictures.

Filmways was owned by Samuel Z. Arkoff, and the company was looking for quality commercial pictures. Arkoff's former distribution group, American International Pictures, had released *Sisters*. *Dressed to Kill* was definitely the kind of product Filmways was seeking. (Ironically, Filmways went bankrupt after *Blow Out* [1981] and the company was bought by Orion Pictures!)

In 1974, Brian De Palma had considered making a film entitled *Cruising*, based on a controversial novel by Gerald Walker about the New York underground gay scene. De Palma abandoned the project for obscure reasons to William Friedkin, but his own script version of *Cruising* gave him the premise for the character played by Angie Dickinson in *Dressed to Kill*.

Friedkin's *Cruising* (1980) is the story of a homosexual psychotic killer who frequents a sadomasochist scene. A cop, played by Al Pacino, goes undercover disguised as a gay man to arrest the killer by setting himself up as prey. At the end, Pacino identifies with the murderer to the point of becoming a practicing homosexual, and—who knows—perhaps also a killer.

Cruising was one of the most controversial films ever released. The gay community felt it depicted homosexuals as corrupt and sick at a time when they were struggling for their rights. Gays tried to stop the shooting of the film and demonstrated in front of theaters where it was playing. The controversy didn't help the film, and *Cruising* was not well received by anyone. *Cruising* did not intentionally put down the gay world; it was only a thriller that took place among a certain group of gay men. The concern, however, was that the public, being misinformed about gay life, might think that the film reflected the entire community. In that sense only was *Cruising* a dangerous film.

De Palma had written a screenplay in 1974 based on the novel that had been published in 1970. De Palma's script was completely different from Friedkin's. The *Cruising* murderer in De Palma's script was a failed actor, a loser who decides to play the role of his life by filming his violence with a video camera. He thinks he is making an important statement about violence.

In his *Cruising* screenplay, De Palma was more intrigued by the killer's amorality, than by making him a pseudo-Freudian homosexual suffering from problems of maladaption—which is the angle Friedkin used. In De Palma's version, the killer at one point murders a gay couple, but he forgets to videotape the crime. When he realizes this, he looks into the camera and says: "I killed them. Both of them. Right in the shower. Just like in *Psycho*. Better than *Psycho*." After this murder, the police assume that the psychopath is gay, and send the Al Pacino character undercover into the gay world. When the murderer finds out about the deduction the police have made, it suddenly destroys his theory of the perfect crime, and to prove them wrong, he murders a woman named Kate. Kate is an insecure housewife; she picks up a stranger in a museum and catches VD from him. Eventually, the killer stabs Kate to death in the elevator of her one-afternoon stand's building.

Evidently, this section in *Cruising* is what became, word-for-word, the setup of *Dressed to Kill*. Kate in *Cruising*, like Kate Miller in *Dressed to Kill*, has wild sexual fantasies. One of them takes place not in a shower, as in the opening sequence of *Dressed to Kill*, but in a football stadium:

> *It's New York Jets-Green Bay Packers Superbowl game. It's very cold. Kate, an attractive young housewife, her husband Mike, and four or five of his business friends huddle under a big glen-plaid blanket. Suddenly everyone jumps as Joe Namath goes back to throw a pass in the closing seconds of the game. The Jets are behind by three points and if Namath doesn't throw a touchdown pass the Jets will lose the game. But he gets a bad pass from the center and is forced to run. As he scrambles backwards, barely missing tacklers coming from all sides, Kate's group turns as a body, wrapped in the blanket, screams with excitement. The man directly behind Kate presses close to her, his breath hot on her neck. She feels his erection through his pants as he signals her with a touch to turn her hips more directly toward him. Kate keeps cheering as Namath eludes more Packers and starts running toward the goal. Everyone goes mad. The man behind Kate has got his cock out and somehow it's between her legs; he tears a hole in her tights under her short skirt and Kate yells louder as the touchdown gets nearer. The group is all jumping up and down, Kate has to lift her legs*

higher, to the next step on the bleachers, to steady herself, allowing the man behind her to slip his cock in her more easily. The whole crowd is leaping frantically now, thumping one another on the back, and the man puts his arm around Kate's shoulder to keep them in rhythm. Kate takes a furtive look toward Mike to see if he realizes what's happening to her. But Mike's attention is riveted on Namath as he crosses the twenty getting ever closer to the goal line. The man is inside Kate now, shot straight up like a ramrod.

KATE AND MAN

All the way, Joe!

They scream together louder than anyone, the two of them leading the excitement like cheerleaders, while Kate feels his cock growing harder and harder, pushing deeper and higher into her with each jump until the cheering for Joe becomes the rhythm of their fucking and all around them everyone is on their side, cheering for them and the touchdown. Kate's excitement gets wilder, almost out of control as she screams for Joe to make it across the goal line. And he does and she screams in a spasm of pleasure—

De Palma then cut to Kate waking, like she does in *Dressed to Kill*, and receiving Mike's "pathetic morning fuck." When De Palma wrote *Dressed to Kill* in 1979, he replaced the knife with a straight razor and the murderer became the victim's shrink.

De Palma's screenplay for *Cruising* was only 87 pages (usually a script runs at least 95 to 100 pages, since one page translates into about one minute on film). This indicates that De Palma intended to make a film where he would favor long visual scenes rather than a lot of dialogue. He retained this concept in *Dressed to Kill*, which is one of his most visually crafted films; there is very little dialogue in the first half hour of the movie, and it's the camera that conveys most of the information about the characters. It is also interesting to note that the screenplays that De Palma has written seldom describe camera movements. De Palma first visualizes his angles in his head, then has them story-boarded, and is ready to shoot.

Brian De Palma wanted *Dressed to Kill* to open with a scene of a man shaving the hair on his body. He shot the sequence with two men pretending to be one person—the first man held the straight razor and the second man got the shave. But the concept was altogether awkward, because the hair on the man's chest wouldn't come off all at once. The scene was abandoned during editing, and Kate's fantasy in the shower became the opening sequence.

INT-BATHROOM-DAY

Mike starts shaving. Kate turns on the water, adjusts the tempera-
ture and steps under the hot spray. She picks up a bar of soap from
the soap dish and slowly moves it across her body. The billowing
steam from the hot water fills the stall, making Mike barely visible
as Kate turns to face him through the glass door. Suddenly Kate is
embraced from behind. She tries to cry out, but a hand is clamped
across her mouth. She feels a man's breath hot on her neck, his
hard cock pressing against her wet ass. He's moving it up between
her legs. Kate gasps for breath, biting down hard on the hand
gripped across her mouth. But the man won't be stopped and Kate
is forced to lift her leg higher, to the ridge on the tile floor, allowing
the man behind her to slip his cock into her. Kate looks wildly at
Mike but he's still shaving completely unaware of what's happening
to her. She grabs frantically at the hand clamped across her mouth,
but the man won't let go, and now it doesn't matter because Kate
feels the cock growing harder and harder, pushing deeper and
higher into her with every move of her struggle. And it doesn't
matter anymore she's fucked by a madman right in front of her
husband because it feels so unbelievably good. Her excitement is
wild, out of control, as she finally manages to pull his hand away
from her mouth and scream out in spasm of pleasure.

De Palma wanted an actress with an old-fashioned look to play the role
of Kate Miller. He offered the project to Liv Ullman, who turned it down—
partly because she found the film too violent. Angie Dickinson got the role
because she physically matched the concept of the character. Michael Caine
was cast as Doctor Elliott. Kate's disturbed psychiatrist. Sean Connery was
also up for the part, but the actor was already tied up with another picture. For
the part of Kate's son, Keith Gordon, who had played the leading role in
Home Movies, was chosen over Matt Dillon and Cameron De Palma (the
director's nephew, who had played the bad kid on his bike screaming, "creepy
Carrie, creepy Carrie!" to Sissy Spacek in the 1976 horror film). Brian De
Palma had written the part of Liz Blake, the "high-class hooker" who
witnesses the murder of Angie Dickinson, for his wife, Nancy Allen. De
Palma wanted his good friend, director Paul Mazursky, to portray the obnoxious Detective Marino, but Mazursky was about to go into production on one
of his own projects. Dennis Franz, who had played a cop in *The Fury*, got the
part instead.

For the shower scene, De Palma hired a body double to replace Angie
Dickinson during the filming of the intimate close-ups. De Palma chose this

alternative only because, since he didn't need to see the actress's face in many shots, it was a way of saving money. Michael Caine was also body doubled in the scenes where he had to appear dressed as a woman. De Palma was concerned that, despite the glasses and the blond wig, the audience would immediately figure out that Caine was the killer. Susanna Clemm, who plays the policewoman in charge of watching Nancy Allen, also portrays Bobbi. For the same reasons, it isn't Michael Caine's voice on his answering machine when he, as Bobbi, calls himself up—it is William Finley's.

Overall, De Palma made only a few changes from the screenplay to the film. In the script, the museum sequence was shorter, and De Palma had planned on having Kate talk to herself while checking out the handsome stranger:

KATE

He's got a lot of nerve trying to pick up such a respectably dressed married women in the middle of the morning—for God sakes! This is a public museum. I have as much right to sit on this bench as he does. Just let him take his eyes off that Picasso and try something. (*Pause*). What's so interesting about that painting? Is it that much more interesting than me?

In the film version, De Palma got rid of the monologue and replaced it with Pino Donaggio's music score, which conveyed the sensuality and the mystery of the chase between Dickinson and the man in the halls of the museum. (Though the film takes place in Manhattan, the interior sequences of the museum were shot in Philadelphia.) De Palma also made a few changes in the last scene of the film. In the screenplay, Nancy Allen didn't see the reflection of the killer in a mirror; instead, she opened the bathroom cabinet and the killer's hand, holding a straight razor, popped out and slashed her throat. Allen woke up from the nightmare in bed with a client. For the film, De Palma obviously changed his mind. Nancy Allen wakes up at Keith Gordon's house. The fact that the young man rushes to her room, instead of being in bed beside her, allows De Palma to close the film on an innocent note, in contrast with the general feeling of the movie.

The first problem that De Palma encountered after he had finished *Dressed to Kill* was with the Motion Picture Association of America. The committee wanted to give to the film an X rating. This meant that no ads could appear in newspapers and that no spots could be aired on television or radio. De Palma had to give in to cutting the most erotic close-ups in the shower scene. He also edited out several shots of the razor slashing up Angie Dickinson and Nancy Allen in the nightmare sequence. De Palma also had to replace the word "cock" with "bulge" when Nancy Allen flirts with Michael Caine.

Dressed to Kill was very unpopular with feminists, who assailed De Palma as being a misogynist, and found the violence against women in his film intolerable and sexist.

Nancy Allen recalled the controversy over *Dressed to Kill*:

> I remember that at the time Brian was very upset. I wasn't as bothered by it as he was, because the controversy brought a lot of attention to the film and gave it extra publicity. About my point of view as a woman on the film and the way it pictures women, I can hardly be objective. I was in the film; Brian had written it for me, so I thought that the women who were against it were just horrible. It's only a movie for God's sake!

In addition to being called a misogynist, De Palma was accused of imitating Hitchcock. Despite the negative response *Dressed to Kill* received from many film critics (Andrew Sarris wrote in the *Village Voice* that the film contained "the same ingredients found in a MacDonald's hamburger"), it also got some fine reviews. Pauline Kael wrote in the *New Yorker*:

> De Palma primes you for what's going to happen and for a lot that doesn't happen. He knows where to put the camera and how to make every move count, and his timing is so great that he gets you every time. His thriller technique, constantly refined, has become insidiously jewelled.

The perfection De Palma achieved with *Dressed to Kill* has so far been unparalleled by any of his other films. *Dressed to Kill* was one of those rare movies that captured the audience's attention and involvement from the first frame, and continued manipulating them with clever and unexpected twists until the end credits. Ralph Bode's photography was superb, and reminiscent of the old-fashioned technicolor Hollywood films. With *Dressed to Kill*, De Palma combined unbearable suspense, eroticism, and sharp violence with a black sense of humor, revealing the director's critical but perceptive view of American society.

Dressed to Kill was a major commercial hit, acknowledging that De Palma had his own distinctive touch, and that he was one of America's leading film directors.

BLOW OUT (1981)

SYNOPSIS: Jack Terri (John Travolta) is a soundman for B movies. One night, as he is recording sounds on a bridge, he witnesses a car accident. Jack rescues one of the passengers, Sally Bedina (Nancy Allen); the other one, presidential candidate Governor McRyan, dies. McRyan's friends beg Jack not to tell anyone that there was a call girl with McRyan in the car. When Jack listens to the tape of the accident, he notices there is a gunshot before the blow out of the tire. He concludes that what he saw was in fact a murder. Jack needs a picture of the accident in sync with his sound to prove his discovery to the police. Sally helps him get the photographs taken by Manny Karp (Dennis Franz) on the scene of the crime. Karp was Sally's accomplice; he was originally supposed to take compromising pictures of McRyan to blackmail him. Jack can now prove that there's been a murder. But Burke (John Lithgow), the killer, destroys all of Jack's evidence except the original, which he intends to intercept when Sally delivers it to Frank Donohue (Curt May), a television reporter. Jack is skeptical, and puts a microphone on Sally to tape the delivery. Sally and the original fall into the hands of Burke. Jack is able to locate the murderer and kill him, but he fails to save Sally. All that Jack has left are Sally's death screams on tape, which he uses on the soundtrack of his latest film.

Among the projects De Palma considered immediately after *Dressed to Kill* was *Act of Vengeance*, a film on the Yablonski murders and the United Mine Workers (the film was eventually made for Home Box Office in 1985, with Charles Bronson and Ellen Burstyn), *Flashdance* for Paramount Pictures (later to be directed by Adrian Lyne), and a thriller called *Personal Effects*, which was renamed *Blow Out*. From his own experience with film students on *Home Movies*, De Palma knew there were many talented young filmmakers waiting for a break in the industry. *Take One*, a film magazine, had organized a contest with De Palma for *Personal Effects*. The magazine published the story line of the film, and the contestants had to come up with the character developments and write two scenes for the picture. The plot at that time was not very different from the final screenplay of *Blow Out*, but was set in Canada instead of Philadelphia, where the movie eventually took place.

(Originally, De Palma wanted to avoid any analogy between the events in the script and the Kennedy/Chappaquiddick affair.)

De Palma's invitation to collaborate with him on *Personal Effects* was tempting, to say the least:

> This is a schematic of a screenplay. I wrote it as a bare plot—the characters, locations, and dramatic situations have little coloring, texture, or emotional development. What I'm looking for is a screenwriter who can take this dramatic framework and create a political thriller. The film should be set in Montreal, and the political context must be Canadian. Even though the plot resonates with past US political events, the film will be a metaphor. I want the screenwriter to create a believable Canadian analogy. This may mean altering certain elements of the treatment. The schematic shows the logic but not the feelings or emotions of the characters. I am especially interested in the development of the scenes between Jon [the name became Jack in the film] and Kate [the name was changed to Sally]. The screenwriter must involve the viewer in the lives of the characters. For instance, what kind of man becomes obsessed with sound effects? What kind of life does he lead, what friends does he have? If the climax of the film is to work, the viewer, through Jon, must have a strong emotional investment in Kate. What feeling does she invoke in him? What kind of woman is she? These are just a few problems the screenwriter will have to solve in the submitted scenes.

Take One promised the winner $500 and the chance to write the screenplay with De Palma. A twenty-six-year-old man was selected from among hundreds of participants, but for obscure reasons, he never collaborated on the writing of the final draft—possibly because by the time he was chosen, *Take One* had gone bankrupt. His name was never mentioned again.

John Travolta had reached a point in his career when he wanted to change his image. He had been considered for the lead in *Prince of the City*, and De Palma chose him to be the star of *Blow Out*. At first, the director was reluctant about having his wife, Nancy Allen, in the film; he was afraid it would hurt her image to only work with her husband. But Travolta, who was a long-time friend of Allen, insisted that she be given the part.

The shoot was long and hard, due to the cold weather in Philadelphia— the city where De Palma had grown up. The director was working for the first time since *The Fury* with a big budget ($18 million) but the production of *Blow Out* was frustrated by a mysterious event: the negative of the scene in which John Travolta crashes through the Liberty Day Parade and drives into a store window, as well as several other inserts, were stolen. A reward was offered to whomever could help trace the film stock. All the calls that the production received were anonymous and misleading, and the film was never found. The entire sequence had to be reshot with insurance money in the spring. Also on the missing reel were some close-ups of the frog Travolta records from the bridge; luckily, inserts were found on other reels.

In *Blow Out*, De Palma paid tribute to his film *Murder a la Mod*, and to *Prince of the City*, a project he felt had been stolen away from him. In one scene in *Blow Out*, Dennis Franz is watching television. Originally, De Palma wanted the character to be watching Francis Coppola's first film, a horror flick entitled *Dementia 13*. But the producer of the movie, Roger Corman, wanted too much money, and De Palma decided instead to use excerpts from *Murder a la Mod* (of a woman walking in a cemetery). De Palma also includes in *Blow Out* a flashback during which John Travolta tells Nancy Allen about his former job—working with cops to denounce corruption in the police force. This was the exact premise of *Prince of the City*.

Blow Out received good reviews, but word of mouth on the film was terrible. The film was assailed for having a downbeat ending (Nancy Allen dies). Many left the theater with the sensation of a sick joke (Travolta uses Allen's screams to dub the film he is working on), feeling drained and deceived. With *Blow Out*, De Palma had tried to move away from graphic violence; Robert Alan Ross from the *Los Angeles Times* noticed De Palma's deliberate effort to find for himself a new identity in the thriller genre: "Don't expect magnificient revelations of gruesome gore from De Palma this time out. But do expect a whopping good time and outstanding contributions from all involved."

Blow Out made about $8 million at the box office, and didn't recoup its high cost, despite the quality of the picture. But perhaps De Palma had overestimated the public, by casting Travolta in a part that didn't match his image, and by giving to *Blow Out* a complicated plot. Basically, with *Blow Out*, De Palma's past experience on *The Fury* repeated itself. But this time around, it didn't alter his image, since his next project was the challenging high budget remake of Howard Hawks's *Scarface*.

SCARFACE *(1983)*

SYNOPSIS: May 1980: Fidel Castro releases 125,000 prisoners and sends them to Miami, Florida. They are all welcomed as survivors of Communism, and the state provides them with money and homes. Tony Montana (Al Pacino) is among the refugees, and he quickly understands that drug dealing might offer a way for him to rise above his mediocre existence. After Montana's first successful but dangerous mission, Frank Lopez (Robert Loggia), the king of cocaine, takes him under his wing. Tony has only one wish, and that is to "have the world and everything in it," including Elvira (Michelle Pfeiffer), Lopez's gorgeous girlfriend. Lopez understands that Montana has the intention of taking over his own kingdom, and tries to eliminate him. He fails, and Tony shoots Lopez in return. Alejandro Sosa (Paul Shenar), a rich dealer, assigns Tony the mission of killing a delegate at the United Nations who is determined to expose the drug connection. But Tony refuses to bring his mission to term when he realizes that he will also have to murder the man's wife and children. Tony's empire falls to pieces. He shoots Manny (Steven Bauer), his best friend, who has secretly married his sister Gina (Mary Elizabeth Mastrantonio), toward whom Tony always had incestuous feelings. Gina and Tony are savagely murdered by Sosa's elite killers, and thus collapses the world of the man best known as Scarface.

The screenplay of *Scarface*, which Oliver Stone wrote in 1983, was a contemporary version of the all-time classic film noir written by Ben Hecht in 1932. Stone had won an Oscar for his screenplay for Alan Parker's *Midnight Express* (1978). Immediately after, he directed his second feature entitled *The Hand* (1981), a horror thriller starring Michael Caine. This effort was an embarrassing critical and financial disaster, and Stone had to retreat to writing screenplays to regain credibility. Oliver Stone wrote *Conan the Barbarian* (1982), *The Year of the Dragon* (1985), and *Scarface*. He returned to directing with *Salvador* (1986), with the Academy Award–winning *Platoon* (1986), and finally with *Wall Street* (1987).

Looking back on the time he worked on *Scarface*, Oliver Stone recalls how the movie got completely out of hand during the filming. *Scarface* was over budget and behind schedule. Money was simply wasted, and Stone remains convinced that *Scarface* could have been done for under the $27 million it cost, without damaging the quality of the film.

Stone felt quite frustrated by De Palma's approach to his screenplay. The director made the scenes longer than they had originally been written by Stone. In consequence, the script had to be cut by at least thirty pages—mostly scenes that involved character development.

Scarface was produced by Martin Bregman for Universal Pictures, and De Palma chose Al Pacino, whom he had considered for the lead in *Blow Out*, to play Tony Montana—alias Scarface. *Scarface* was, for Pacino, his biggest challenge since *The Godfather Part II* (1974); after that, most of the films he had appeared in had received little notice. With *Scarface*, the actor wanted to prove he was as good as his rivals, Robert De Niro and Dustin Hoffman, who were after the same roles as he was—and getting them.

Conflicts again erupted when *Scarface* was screened for the Motion Picture Association of America. The word "fuck" and its variations were used repeatedly in the dialogue, but most of all, the board thought that the film was too graphic and violent.

Martin Bregman openly accused Richard Heffner, the chairman of the seven-person rating board of the MPAA, of having a vendetta against De Palma because he had publicly complained about Heffner's treatment of *Dressed to Kill*. Heffner simply responded by saying: "We aren't waging a vendetta against Mr. De Palma. I never considered anything he said a personal attack. We rate films, not their makers!"

To avoid the X rating, De Palma cut a close-up to satisfy the MPAA. The director later declared to Playboy: "I didn't take [out] anything except the arm that was chain-sawed off!"

The press on the film was mixed. Pauline Kael, who had been a frank supporter of De Palma, wrote: "*Scarface* has the length of an epic but not the texture of an epic and its dramatic arc is faulty!" On the other hand, Vincent Canby found *Scarface* as memorable as *The Godfather*. Despite the gigantic ad campaign Universal had invested, *Scarface* made only as much as it had cost.

Scarface is, perhaps, De Palma's least personal movie. Nothing in it really has the originality or the visuals that characterize his style, and set him apart from the directors for hire. *Scarface* lacks emotions; it lacks the artist's vision—and possibly also his motivation—behind it. *Scarface* was a well done, well acted, empty film with no identity. Though *Scarface* hardly qualified for the "hit" category, it had now established Brian De Palma as a Hollywood director.

A screenplay entitled *Fire* had been chosen as De Palma's next challenge. The director had written the first draft of the screenplay in 1982.

Somewhat inspired by the life of Jim Morrison, the story concerns Jake DeNardo, a rock 'n' roll star who, the world believed, had died in a car crash. A journalist named Dave Barrish thinks he sees DeNardo alive and well in Brazil. Calling on his past experiences with the controversial *Dionysus in '69*, De Palma made DeNardo a member of an actor's troupe who plays *Dionysus*. He used this device to set up a crisis in DeNardo's life:

> *Dionysus (DeNardo) starts to dance in the center of the circle. One by one, the other group members join him as though they're caught up with his erotic spell. Others get instruments—a flute, tambourines, temple bells, conga drums—and begin to play them, creating a savage throbbing music. Members of the audience start to join the actors until the garage is transformed into a primitive discothèque. The group members take off their clothes and the audience follows their lead. Soon the room is vibrating with hot, naked bodies moving erotically, obsessively, madly to the beat of the drum. Jake watches from his tower above. He's never seen anything like this before. The mood in the room is ecstatic chaos—yet there's nothing violent about it. Everybody's having a great time.*

Later in his career, during a concert, DeNardo brings a girl on stage from the audience and simulates a sexual act in front of a delirious crowd. The singer is then accused of having raped the girl on stage and, despite the lack of evidence, he is sentenced to prison. The accusation had been partly set up by a young filmmaker whose wife had had an affair with DeNardo; he has the concert on film. DeNardo refuses to let himself be the victim of an injustice, and decides to fake his death in a car accident. The screenplay was structured in flashbacks, and the journalist puts together the pieces of the mystery, finally deciding not to reveal that DeNardo is still alive.

Fire would have been a film in the vein of *The Rose* (1979). Producer Keith Barish wanted to do the picture with Twentieth Century Fox (the distributor of *The Rose*). John Travolta had been set to play DeNardo, and had arranged to go on a two-month tour with a rock band. But Barish suddenly dropped the project because he considered the script exceedingly flawed. It's possible that De Palma will eventually decide to return to *Fire* but there will then be the matter of finding a studio, and also a producer, who will either be satisfied with the script or have enough faith in the project to convince De Palma to rewrite it.

In 1984, De Palma directed a video clip featuring his favorite rock star, Bruce Springsteen (many of Springsteen's songs were supposed to be in *Fire*), performing in concert his hit song "Dancing in the Dark." At the end of the song, Springsteen pulls a young girl from the audience onto the stage and starts dancing with her. This ending was De Palma's tribute—and possibly farewell—to *Fire*.

BODY DOUBLE (1984)

SYNOPSIS: Jake Scully (Craig Wasson) is cursed; his acting is put in jeopardy when he has a claustrophobic attack while shooting a vampire film, and he finds out that his girlfriend is cheating on him. Jake meets Sam Bouchard (Gregg Henry), also an actor, who offers to let Jake stay in a gorgeous house while he goes to Seattle for a play. Sam tells Jake that every night, at the same time, Gloria Revelle (Deborah Shelton), the woman next door, performs a masturbation ritual. Jake is thrilled, and peeps on the woman until he realizes that a man, who he thinks is an American Indian, is also watching her. The next day, Jake sees the same Indian following Gloria from a shopping mall to a beach motel, where he steals her purse. Jake runs after him and the pursuit climaxes in a tunnel; Jake has another claustrophobic attack, and he gets the purse but is unable to stop the Indian. Gloria helps Jake recover from the chase and they fall into each other's arms. The woman suddenly resists and runs away. Jake is calling Gloria to apologize when he sees that the Indian is in her house. But it's too late for Jake to do anything—Gloria is murdered with an electric drill. The detective (Guy Boyd) in charge of the case does not like Jake— after all, Jake is a Peeping Tom. Later, while watching the X-rated television channel, Jake connects a masturbation routine performed by porn queen Holly Body (Melanie Griffith) with Gloria's. Jake purposely gets cast to star with Holly in her new film and elicits from her the confession that Sam Bouchard had hired her to imper-sonate Gloria. Finally, Jake also discovers that Sam was the Indian. Jake had been set up to witness a murder committed by someone who didn't exist! Jake fights his phobia, kills Sam, and saves him-self as well as Holly from being buried alive. Jake has become a hero, and can now assume this role both on the screen and in real life.

De Palma was angry about the way *Dressed to Kill* and *Scarface* had been forced back to the cutting room by the MPAA. With *Body Double*, he wanted to show how far more suggestive he could get. De Palma declared: "I have a project called *Body Double* and I'm going to make it an X movie," he declared. "You wanna see violence? You wanna see sex? I think it's about time to blow the top off the ratings!"

Originally, De Palma had wanted to produce *Body Double*, and had hired Ken Wiederhorn to direct it. But *Scarface* was not a hit, and *Fire* had gone up in smoke, so De Palma needed to get a project going. He decided to take back *Body Double* and direct the film himself, leaving behind a quite angry Ken Wiederhorn, who said:

> De Palma had seen my film *Eyes of a Stranger* (1981) and liked it. He called me and said he was tired of doing thrillers but wanted to produce one called *Body Double*. I agreed to do it, only if he allowed me to hire a writer to work on the script. I love De Palma's films, but I don't think his plots make sense. I wanted *Body Double* to have a very good story. He said I would be in control of the film. But De Palma was in the middle of a crisis. *Scarface* had cost a lot of money and it was not a success. Columbia Pictures said they would do *Body Double* only if De Palma directed it. He jumped on the occasion because he was afraid no other company would want to work with him after he had brought *Scarface* over budget. He asked his agent, Marty Bauer, to call me to tell me I was fired. De Palma is pretty much the man you imagine him to be when you see his films. The first time I met him, he said "you got the job, but we don't have to be friends!"

Body Double was written by Robert J. Avrech and Brian De Palma, based on a story by De Palma. Originally set in Manhattan, the location of the story was changed to Los Angeles, possibly to avoid the connection with Hitchcock's *Rear Window* (1954). The murderer in the script was disguised as a Rastafarian, but De Palma changed that to an American Indian. In the screenplay, Gloria was drowned in her bathtub. De Palma decided to stay away from another shower scene, and settled for an execution with an electric drill. At the end of the original script, the hero had a final confrontation with the murderer in a swimming pool; once the Rastafarian fell in the water, his make-up was washed away and his true identity was finally revealed. De Palma also decided to explain—through the concept of a film within a film—

the title, *Body Double*, at the end, when originally it was explained in the opening sequence.

De Palma wanted to push the inevitable controversy to the boiling point by casting porn queen Annette Haven to play the role of Holly Body, but she finally lost the part to Melanie Griffith.

Craig Wasson, who rehearsed for the part with the porn actress, said:

> Annette is very serious and committed to her profession, because she's been attacked morally so many times. She had to find a way to defend herself and explain why she was doing that kind of work. The result of all of this is that she's built up a shell and you could feel it while rehearsing for the role. . . . That's why she lost the part.

Melanie Griffith is the daughter of Tippi Hedren, Hitchcock's discovery for *The Birds* (1963), who also had the lead in the all-time classic *Marnie* (1964), opposite Sean Connery. Griffith was married to Steven Bauer, who played Al Pacino's right hand man in *Scarface*. She had first met De Palma when he was casting *Carrie*. "He wanted me to kiss that guy that I didn't know," recalled Griffith ironically. "I said I didn't want to do it. Brian simply told me to get out. I said fine, goodbye and that was it!"

De Palma wanted to cast actress Jamie Lee Curtis (whose mother, Janet Leigh, had also worked with Hitchcock on *Psycho*) to play Holly Body, but she refused because she had already played too many hookers on film and was afraid that one more shot at it would typecast her for the rest of her career. So Griffith accepted the role opposite Craig Wasson.

Craig Wasson, relating his experience of his first meeting with De Palma, said:

> There was a line in that scene when I go to an audition and sit in front of all these people. One was asking me: "Tell us something about yourself, something that really means a lot to you emotionally." I was supposed to answer: "Well, I just caught my girlfriend in bed with that guy's dick in her mouth." Anyway, when I first met Brian he said to me: "Well, how is everything? Are you married?" I answered: "Not exactly. . . ." He replied: "What happened?" and that's when I gave him the line from the screenplay. He liked that because I got the part, but the line was cut from the dialogue . . ."

When *Body Double* came out, it hardly got the controversial attention De Palma expected—and wanted—it to receive. The film was playing against Ken Russell's *Crimes of Passion*; this time around, it was the Russell film that was threatened with an X rating by the MPAA.

Body Double was not successful, and De Palma recalled feeling "shell shocked. I just sat in my room and stared at the wall." The reviews went from one extreme to another. *"Body Double* is just twice as terrible," wrote Rex Reed in the *New York Post*. *Newsday* titled its review: "De Palma Overdose." The film also found supporters like Jack Kroll, who wrote in *Newsweek*: "De Palma has never been more brilliant!"

Although *Body Double* was a well-crafted film it was far from being a success. De Palma was angry at the board of censorship and the critics when he made it, and his excessive, unmotivated use of violence and explicit sexuality almost seemed a defiant act against his detractors and this emotional involvement on the director's part impaired his judgement. Regardless of the reasons, his failure with *Body Double* kept him away from thrillers for a while.

WISE GUYS *(1986)*

SYNOPSIS: Harry Valentini (Danny DeVito) and Moe Dickstein (Joe Piscopo) have been best friends since childhood and are active members of the New Jersey mob scene. Harry and Moe get in trouble when they bet all of their boss's money on the wrong horse at a race. They both receive separately the order to kill one another. In order to avoid this mission, Harry seeks the help of his Uncle Mike in Atlantic City. But he finds out that the poor man has died. Fortunately, Harry's grandmother has kept quite a fortune, which she gives to the pair to pay their debts. In the meantime, Frank "the Fixer" (Captain Lou Albano), Moe and Harry's worst enemy, realizes that they've used his credit cards to the limit and have smashed his pink Cadillac. Bobby DiLea (Harvey Keitel), a retired gangster who has become the "Ceasar" of Atlantic City, manages to calm Frank down for the sake of his friendship with Harry's family. Harry subsequently decides to gamble with his grandmother's money and Moe, out of desperation, shoots his best friend. Later, Moe has decided to kill himself when suddenly, Harry reappears—his death had only been staged. The pair succeed at last in slaying their enemies. Together, they open an Italian/Jewish deli.

Wise Guys is a comedy in the vein of *Get to Know Your Rabbit*. With this film, De Palma hoped to surprise both the audience and the critics by doing a conventional comedy.

De Palma's experience with MGM, the distributor of *Wise Guys*, mirrored the bad experience he'd had with Warner on *Rabbit*. After holding back the film, MGM finally released it and surprisingly, *Wise Guys* got an honest response from the critics and from the audience.

MGM organized a press conference to publicize the film, which was conducted appropriately enough, in a restaurant in Manhattan's Little Italy. De Palma sat at the center of attention, not wholly disguising his boredom. After the media barrage, there was an opportunity to talk to the director privately.

De Palma came off as a sharp, serious, academic, and reticent man. Here, in part, is the interview:

Laurent Bouzereau:

From 1963 until 1973 you directed comedies; then, for the next ten years you only did thrillers. Now you're back with a comedy. Is this a new beginning?

Brian De Palma:

Well, one always hope so! I think it's important to try to do more and more challenging and new things. In order to do that, you have to work a lot and be able to learn from your past experiences, the good as well as the bad ones.

LB: Do you feel more comfortable directing screenplays that you wrote or scripts written by someone else?

BD: I basically like to do both. It can be dangerous to keep working on your own stuff. It can become very tiring. You also have to watch out you don't start repeating yourself.

LB: You sure didn't repeat yourself with *Wise Guys* . . .

BD: This time, no one can accuse me of ripping off Hitchcock.

LB: Does this accusation affect you?

BD: It certainly does.

LB: Why? Do you think it's not a fair statement?

BD: It's a tired perception. I've noticed that most of the people who keep accusing me of basing my movies on Hitchcock's don't even know his work well. It becomes really upsetting after a while.

LB: Do you prefer to scare your audience or "to make 'em laugh"?

BD: Do I prefer to scare them or to make them laugh? . . . [*long pause*] I guess I like to do both. Yes, that's right, I like to do both.

LB: What is the movie that marked you when you were younger and that never left you since then?

BD: *Bambi!* I'll never forget that moment before Bambi's mother gets shot; it was terrifying. *Dumbo* also had a pretty strong effect on me when I was a kid.

LB: In *Body Double*, Craig Wasson explains to the cop that he found out that it's the husband of the victim who hired an Indian to kill his wife. You see visually the husband and the Indian. This scene is impossible because we then find out that they were the same person. Why did you lie to the audience by filming what couldn't have happened?

BD: Well, I didn't really lie to the audience because when the scene happens, it is supposed to be what the character played by Craig Wasson thinks is the truth. I don't find the scene misleading.

LB: Then what about the scene in *Sisters* during which Margot Kidder talks to the shadow of her sister when at the end we discover she had been dead all that time?

BD: [*Laughs*] I admit it, I cheated a little bit in this case! I remember we used a dummy in the scene. I never felt bad about doing it!

LB: In *Dressed to Kill* you used Michael Caine dressed as a woman outside the museum before his part as the killer could be known. This became a role essential to the story. Since this detail can only be caught at a second viewing of the films, why did you do it?

BD: I think it's because I like to give a lot of subtext to my films. The detail you just mentioned is meant to be caught by a very limited amount of people, but I still think it's important that it exists.

LB: Do you like to deal with the Hollywood studios?

BD: I LOVE THE STUDIOS! [*screaming and stretching out his arms*] So many of them! I love them all!

LB: Among all the films you've directed, which one is your favorite?

BD: People have often asked me this question. It's kind of hard to answer because first of all, I don't sit home and watch my films. The vision you have of your work also changes as you grow older. There are some films that I don't really care for anymore, some that surprise me like *Scarface* or *Phantom of the Paradise*. I don't know why but I have a tendency to like the less successful ones. . . . .

LB: You read Stephen King's *Carrie* and it became one of your most successful films. Did you feel at the time that King would become as popular as he is now?

BD: I think that no one can predict one's future in this business. For my taste, *Carrie* is his best novel, even though I find the book a little overwritten.

LB: How do you feel when people accuse you of being a misogynist?

BD: This argument is as passé as the one about Hitchcock.

LB: A few years ago you almost directed a remake of *Treasure of the Sierra Madre* with Steven Spielberg. What happened?

BD: We are still thinking of doing something together. We have several projects we would like to work on.

LB: What do you think of Spielberg's ascendancy in the industry?

BD: I think he is a real genius. I loved *ET*; it is a masterpiece.

LB: But you said in an interview: "I've seen Steven working day in and day out on *ET* toys. It's real bad. I'm a creative person. Why would I want to worry about designing *ET* lamps?"

BD: I was only referring to this specific example and not to his talent as a director. I even liked *1941* a lot, though he got a little carried away with that one!

LB: Film critics don't treat your work very well. Are you the kind of director who gets affected by bad reviews?

BD: Of course. No one likes to be criticized. But I do believe that what counts is to do films that are true to you. I do movies with my own instinct. I try to do what I think is right. Film critics have a power over filmgoers. Even *I* read them to choose the films I want to see. But in the end, the ultimate arbitrators are not the critics or the audience. The ultimate arbitrator is time. The test of time will decide which movies will last forever. I think that some films that were successful when they were released won't survive and will seem ridiculous. Just take the example of Cecil B. DeMille; I find him impossible to watch. You laugh your way through his films!

LB: What lies in the future of Brian De Palma?

BD: I hope more challenges and many more movies! I am currently working on the screen adaptation of the TV series *The Untouchables* for Paramount Pictures. I'm also developing a screenplay entitled *Carpool* [*Note*: As reported by Martin Amis in *Vanity Fair* of November 1984, with *Carpool*, De Palma intends to indulge his fascination with rear view mirrors and expects at last to get an X rating.] I also want to direct a stage adaptation for Broadway of

Phantom of the Paradise, with a new approach and a totally different cast and crew.

THE UNTOUCHABLES (1987)

SYNOPSIS: Chicago 1931. Prohibition. A bar is bombed, killing an innocent girl. Eliot Ness (Kevin Costner), a young and ambitious federal agent, resolves to start a war against Al Capone (Robert De Niro). After a misfire, Ness decides to create his own gang with three men: James Malone (Sean Connery), an arrogant cop, Oscar Wallace (Charles Martin Smith), an accountant, and George Stone (Andy Garcia), a sharpshooter. Together, they become "the Untouchables." They stop a convoy of alcohol at the Canadian border, and decide that the only way to arrest Capone is to prove that he hasn't paid taxes on most of his income. After Wallace is killed as a warning, Ness hesitates to go on; he is afraid for his family. But Malone learns that Capone's accountant, who is carrying a compromising ledger listing his boss's illicit earnings, can be intercepted at the train station. Malone pays the price of this information with his own life. A shooting perfectly orchestrated by Ness and Stone leads to the arrest of Capone's accountant. During the trial, Frank Nitty (Billy Drago), Capone's hit man, gives him a list of names. Suspicious, Ness asks to search Nitty and consequently finds proof that he is responsible for Malone's death. After a merciless pursuit, Ness finally kills Nitty and comes back to the courtroom. Capone has paid off the members of the jury to decide in his favor, but Ness defeats this last-ditch effort. Ness celebrates his victory and finds out that the law against prohibition may soon be abolished. . . .

Paramount Pictures had also offered Brian De Palma the chance to direct a film entitled *Fatal Attraction*. De Palma rejected the project for the same reasons John Carpenter had turned it down: *Fatal Attraction* was a rip-off of Clint Eastwood's *Play Misty for Me*. (It seems unfair that the critics who immediately point out the parallels between De Palma's films and Hitchcock's rarely mention that *Fatal Attraction* is little more than a remake of *Misty*. If De Palma had chosen to direct *Fatal Attraction*, there's little doubt he would have immediately incurred criticism for misogyny and plagiarism.)

Art Linson, the producer of the Academy Award-winning *Melvin and Howard*, brought De Palma David Mamet's screen version of *The Untouch-*

ables. Mamet, who is a Pulitzer prize-winning playwright (*Glengarry Glen Ross*) and screenwriter (his credits include *The Verdict* and the recent remake of *The Postman Always Rings Twice*), had worked with Linson for eight months on developing the script and doing research on prohibition. Brian De Palma was Linson's first choice to direct *The Untouchables*. Linson recalls:

> I wanted De Palma because he makes things look important and at the same time he's great with action. For the first time, he's been given a screenplay that has a lot of heart and sentiment. It might be the first De Palma movie where audiences cry at the end. He's always amazed you, he's always scared the shit out of you, he's always pummeled you and he's always made you feel that he's a brilliant filmmaker—but you didn't always love the movies or love the characters. I know women who walked out of *Scarface* and wouldn't see *Body Double* who go up to him afterward and say, "Oh, Brian"—and this is a pretty violent movie. But it doesn't seem violent because you love the characters so much.

The budget on *The Untouchables* was set at $16 million; at the end of production, it had gone beyond $24 million. Money became critical when it came time to film the climactic train station sequence; it was the last scene scheduled to be shot. Art Linson describes the scene:

> Brian invented the stairs scene, aided by a slight homage to Eisenstein's *Potemkim*. That was started by an economic problem—the original shootout was to take place somewhere else under a different set of circumstances, but it was too expensive. If you gave this puzzle to all the directors in America, I don't think anybody could have solved it as well as Brian, except maybe Steven Spielberg: "Brian, we're out of money. Sorry, the moving trains, the helicopter shots, we can't do it. You have the stairs, some extras and some guns—make it exciting, give us something we haven't seen before because it's your final big set-piece of the movie." And he came up with his exciting fifteen minutes of film with just a staircase and a big clock. To be on the side of that is to really appreciate Brian.

Kevin Costner was chosen to play the role of Eliot Ness; Mel Gibson, among others, had also been considered for the part. Sean Connery joined the film as Malone, Ness's best friend. De Palma had three actors in mind to play Al Capone: British actor Bob Hoskins, Al Pacino, and Robert De Niro. De Niro was not available and so Hoskins was finally chosen over Pacino to portray Capone. Shortly before the shooting started, De Niro declared that he he wanted the role . . . for $1.5 million (De Palma got the same salary to direct the picture). Linson suddenly found himself in an embarrassing situation. "For the first time in my life," he said, "I was in the position of a football manager who has a good quarterback and all of a sudden there's this opportunity to bring a great one in . . ."

Bob Hoskins was subsequently paid $200,000 for his trouble, and De Niro was reunited with De Palma for the first time since *Hi, Mom!* in 1970.

The Untouchables was instantly a hit. It was released on June 5, 1987, in 1,012 theaters, and it grossed $10,023,094 on its opening weekend. Sean Connery, who also received a Golden Globe Award in the same category, received an Oscar for Best Supporting Actor. Other Oscar nominations for this film included Ennio Morricone for Best Music; Marilyn Vance for Best Costume Designer; Hal Gausman for Best Set Direction; Patrizia Von Brandenstein and William A. Elliott for Art Direction. Absent is the Academy's recognition of De Palma's direction—but then, Hitchcock never won an Oscar. Even though Paramount Pictures purposefully played down De Palma's role of director in their ad campaign for *The Untouchables*, the director's brilliance is all over the film, and it cannot be separated out from its broad appeal and popularity. This film is a breakthrough for De Palma.

So effective was their relationship that producer Art Linson and De Palma have teamed up again for another film, which is in production at the writing of this book. *Casualties of War*, currently being shot in the Philippines, stars Michael J. Fox and Sean Penn. Despite some well established Vietnam War classics, such as Coppola's *Apocalypse Now*, Stone's *Platoon*, and Kubrick's *Full Metal Jacket*, De Palma told *Rolling Stone* "none of them have had really great stories. This is a great story, based on a real incident."

The screenplay, written by David Rabe, who wrote the successful play *Hurlyburly*, is based on a novel by Daniel Lang (1969). The story is set in 1966 and focusses on an American soldier's dilemma: should he remain loyal to the four men in his outfit whom he witnesses kidnap, rape, and murder a Vietnamese girl, or should he report the crime. His decision and its consequences make *Casualties of War* a riveting story—one that may well finally match the director's riveting style.

FOUR

The ultimate challenge for a director is to be able to create and impose his own style—the *je ne sais quoi* that sets apart the artist from the director for hire. Very few contemporary directors have managed to both achieve commercial success and retain artistic credibility. The two elements are rarely compatible. Many directors whose movies have been highly successful—such as Richard Donner, who made *The Omen* (1976), *Superman* (1978), and *Lethal Weapon* (1987)—are seldom acknowledged as artists. Brian De Palma has achieved his place in the film industry by being artistically independent first, and then slowly managing to slip his distinctive style into his commercial pictures. Many Hollywood filmmakers begin their careers by doing exploitation movies (slashers, low budget horror, etc.) that hardly leave room to develop inventive concepts, but rather serve the express purpose as audition material to land a contract as director with a studio. Once there, the director is often controlled by producers, who are necessarily favoring the stars, and the director's artistic potentional can never develop. De Palma came at the industry on an oblique angle. His early films, largely social satires, are filled with the risk-taking necessary to develop an original style. Once he found it—he never let it go.

When De Palma made *Dressed to Kill*, *Blow Out*, and *Body Double*, his name alone was used in ad campaigns for the films. Trailers and posters announced the new movie by the modern master of suspense and of the macabre. Conversely, when De Palma made big budget films like *Scarface* and *The Untouchables*, the distributors built the campaigns around the stars of the films. It seems obvious that the name of Brian De Palma has become both a blessing and a curse to his films. Though his style is always recognizable, the major producers evidently fear that the controversy surrounding some of De Palma's films might hurt the box office results of his more mainstream movies.

Brian De Palma has developed his craft from film to film. His style has gone from nervous, high speed, jump cut pacing to more slow and descriptive visuals. His first movies were influenced by the French New Wave, but he slowly gave up hand carried camera shots for sophisticated travelings. But in all cases, De Palma has kept a creative and unusual touch.

In the films of Brian De Palma, it is often the camera, rather than the dialogue, that tips off the audience to plot elements and makes them feel the entanglements inside the characters' psyches. For example, in *Dressed to Kill*, when the character played by Angie Dickinson wakes up in the apartment of the man she met at the museum, she dresses while the camera slowly retreats into the living room. The actress is still the center of our attention when the camera pans slightly toward the phone on a table. As she is about to leave the room, Dickinson hesitates and looks back at the phone, just as the camera finishes panning on it. Dickinson walks to it and calls her husband. What is most fascinating about this scene is that we anticipate the character's behavior only because the camera panned to the phone. In the same sequence, when Angie Dickinson is on the bed, putting on her bracelets, the camera focuses for a split second on her wedding ring, which she has left on a modern alarm clock. Subconsciously, this focus makes the audience uneasy. This serves as a way for De Palma to build up suspense. The audience anticipates the moment when the character realizes that she has forgotten her ring.

By giving out as much visual information as possible, Brian De Palma encourages his audience to participate in the action of the film. He wants the spectators to become actively involved with the characters' intimate worlds. The split screen is probably De Palma's most original concept. He has persistently used this method to present his plot from several angles, or to express two actions happening simultaneously.

The genesis of De Palma's use of the split screen technique appears in his first film *The Wedding Party*: three men (Robert De Niro, William Finley, and

Charles Pfluger) walk first on one side and then on the other of a row of trees. The camera changes point of view each time the men are either to the left or to the right of the trees. De Palma included the exact same shot in *Greetings*, this time with De Niro, Gerrit Graham, and Jonathan Worden walking between the columns of a building. In *Carrie*, De Palma filmed a young boy riding his bicycle between trees the same way he had shot the two scenes previously mentioned.

Eventually instead of disrupting his image by switching points of view, the director decided to present the different shots on a split screen. In 1969, De Palma used three cameras to film the controversial play *Dionysus in '69*. The play was presented as an image divided in three parts. By offering different perspectives, De Palma placed the audience in a position to judge the action from the point of view of the public as well as of the actors on stage.

De Palma used the device of the split screen to the same effect in several of his films. The murder of Margot Kidder's lover in *Sisters* is seen from the room the man is in, and also from the window of the woman who witnesses the killing (Jennifer Salt). The action is actually shown from the perspective of both a peeper (Salt) and a peeped (the victim). Later, when the police question Margot Kidder at the door to her apartment, De Palma avoids the usual angle reverse between the characters by showing on the left side of the screen, the action as seen from the corridor, and on the right side, the action as viewed from inside the apartment. In *Phantom of the Paradise*, the Phantom (William Finley) spies on the rehearsal of a song from the balcony of the theater. The action is shown from both his perspective and from the point of view of the performers on stage—where the Phantom has placed a bomb. We can feel both Phantom's excitement, and the growing danger of the actors on stage. When Sissy Spacek transforms the prom in *Carrie* into a blood bath, the intensity of her evil powers is translated by the split screen, which simultaneously offers many different views of the chaos.

De Palma also used the split screen to show two actions taking place at the same time, but in different places. In *Sisters*, while William Finley is cleaning up after the murder in Margot Kidder's apartment, Jennifer Salt is trying to convince the police that she witnessed the killing. In *Dressed to Kill*, Nancy Allen and Michael Caine are both watching, in their separate apartments, the same TV show (Phil Donahue's interview with a transsexual). Later, when the policewoman peeps on Allen, De Palma filmed the scene on a split screen. On one side, the blond officer watches Allen, and on the other side, Michael Caine listens to a message on his answering machine left by

Bobbi, the killer. In this scene, De Palma uses the split screen device to mislead his audience, so we don't suspect that Bobbi is, in fact, Michael Caine.

Finally, De Palma uses the split screen to show what a character thinks. In *Dressed to Kill*, the second half of the screen reveals to us when Angie Dickinson remembers, in the museum, that the man who's been following her has her glove. The same device is used when the character remembers leaving her underwear in the cab she took with the man from the museum, and also when she realizes she's forgotten her ring in the man's apartment, and sees herself putting it on the alarm clock. In *Blow out*, when John Travolta listens to the recording of the car accident, he realizes that in addition to the blow out of the tire, he hears the sound of a gunshot. On one side of the screen, we see John Travolta listening to his tape, and on the second half we see his mental reconstruction of the accident.

By multiplying the images, De Palma reveals twice as much information about his plots and his characters. Ultimately, the split screen is De Palma's tribute to film; it proves that an image can have several dimensions and an action, when seen from different perspectives, can have multiple implications and meanings. The split screen imbues the audience with the feeling of living an action from a very objective point of view—they can choose whichever angle they want. The split screen in this sense is a technique that gives the spectator the freedom to take a position.

Brian De Palma often centers his plots around film people or around characters who are exploring visual arts. Sometimes, they try to use their knowledge of film to solve the conflicts in their lives. By taking his audience behind the scenes of filmmaking, as in *Blow Out* and *Body Double*, Brian De Palma is like a magician who gives away his tricks, but is still able to manipulate and surprise his audience. But ultimately, the concept of films about film shows how thoroughly he understands the technical side of moviemaking, and how much he wants to share it by inserting it into his plots.

De Palma's visual concepts are the marriage of images and technical virtuosity. He relies almost exclusively on what images can tell, as in a silent film, but he amplifies his visual statements by employing his technical brilliance. Thereby, he is able to communicate plot elements, characters' secret wishes, and the overall mood of the film without dialogue.

In *Carrie*'s climactic prom scene, immediately after Sissy Spacek and William Katt have been elected Queen and King, Amy Irving realizes that a rope travels from underneath the stage to the top of a scaffolding and is connected to a bucket, filled with blood. We hear the clapping of the students and teachers cheering Spacek and Katt, but the camera follows the rope the same way Amy Irving does. Suddenly, Nancy Allen pulls the rope and the bucket showers Spacek with blood. At this point, the only sounds we hear are the bucket clanking at the end of the rope and the blood dripping. By reducing the sound effects in this whole sequence, De Palma has reinforced the shocking climax and has focused our attention on a visual expectation. When the bucket is finally free of the rope and hits William Katt on the head, the screams and laughter of the teachers and the students return. In this sequence, De Palma gives sound a dramatic effect. The contrast—silence juxtaposed with the hysterical and loud mockery of Carrie's enemies—contributes to the intensity of the moment.

In his first movies, *The Wedding Party* and *Greetings*, De Palma was already giving priority to images over dialogue—he even used title cards between the segments, as in the era of the silent movies. Later, in *The Fury*, when Amy Irving escapes from the institute where she is kept prisoner, in *Dressed to Kill*, when Angie Dickinson picks up a man in a museum, and in *The Untouchables*, on the steps of a train station, De Palma continued to express action without the support of any dialogue.

Slow motion and fast motion are two devices that De Palma often uses to create palpable suspense, to attract our attention to details, or to give comic relief. The first sequence of *The Wedding Party* is in fast motion. A young man arrives to visit his future in-laws. His financée's family picks him up at the ferry station. The sequence is made totally crazy by the excitement of the moment; the mother-in-law-to-be insists on driving and creates a big commotion. The fast motion reflects the feelings of the guest, and also communicates immediately to the audience the genre of the picture—a comedy. When the young man is finally introduced to the rest of the family in the following sequence, De Palma suddenly breaks the rhythm by switching abruptly from fast to slow motion. This contrast is what makes the audience realize the young man's embarrassment; the family of his bride-to-be is snobby, and appraises the future husband in the most obvious way. The slow motion reflects the young man's feeling that the introduction is never going to end. It also reveals that the wedding party is about to become an uncomfortable experience for the groom.

De Palma used fast motion for comic relief in the scene in *Carrie* where

William Katt and two of his friends are trying on suits for the prom. One of them refuses to wear a tuxedo, and the comedy of the argument escalates when the scene suddenly changes to fast motion. The juxtaposition of this heightened humor with the horror that almost immediately follows makes the latter's impact all the more powerful.

Fast motion shots also appear in *Hi, Mom!*, *Home Movies*, and *Phantom of the Paradise*. In both *Hi, Mom!* and *Home Movies*, De Palma filmed scenes of a couple making love in fast motion. The device conveys the casualness of the acts. This device may even have inspired Stanley Kubrick, who filmed fast motion lovemaking sequences in *A Clockwork Orange* (1971), a year after *Hi, Mom!* was made. Kubrick explained to French critic Michel Ciment that he had made this choice to show the sexual act as a banal ritual rather than as a passionate encounter. His description applies equally well to De Palma's use of fast motion. Conversely, each time Keith Gordon sees Nancy Allen in *Home Movies*, she is filmed in slow motion. The contrast between fast and slow motion reveals visually that Gordon has fallen in love with Allen. In *Phantom of the Paradise*, the fast motion sequences give the film a satirical mood rather than establishing a strong contrast; they remind us that, although the story is dramatic, *Phantom of the Paradise* is a parody that goes beyond a simple horror story.

The climax of *Blow Out*, during which John Travolta tries to save Nancy Allen, is shot in slow motion. This device enables us to foresee that Travolta won't rescue Allen this time (he had saved her from drowning at the beginning of the film). The slow motion gives an immediate indication that Travolta has become powerless, and will arrive too late to save Allen from being murdered.

In *Obession*, the last scene is in slow motion as well. At this point in the film, Cliff Robertson still doesn't know that Genevieve Bujold is his daughter; he is determined to kill her. When Bujold sees Robertson, she runs toward him. Because De Palma shoots this action in slow motion, the audience has time to wonder whether Robertson is going to kill her. The slow motion builds up to the moment when Bujold finally falls into Robertson's arms, and calls him "daddy." At this point, De Palma switches from slow to normal motion, reflecting the resolution of conflicts—the lives of both characters have also returned to normal.

Rather than cutting back and forth between what goes on in the background and what is shown in the foreground, De Palma often likes to present both perspectives in focus simultaneously. This device allows him to make the audience feel the action and also anticipate the reactions of the characters.

In *Carrie*, the teacher reads a poem to the class; he announces that William Katt wrote it. Katt is in focus in the foreground, Sissy Spacek is in focus in the background. When the teacher asks for comments, we instinctively know that Carrie is going to express her feelings about the young man's poem, and that she is probably the only one who paid attention to it. The emphasis that De Palma draws in this sequence, by having both actors in focus, also foreshadows the developments in Carrie's relationship with her classmate.

In *Home Movies*, Keith Gordon goes to see a lawyer to get advice on his mother's divorce case. While sitting in the waiting area, he overhears a telephone conversation between the receptionist and a client, and it gives him the idea of filming his father cheating on his wife. The scene is shot with both characters in focus, though they are sitting at opposite ends of the room. This points out that Gordon is listening to the receptionist, and focuses our attention on what this minor character is saying. The focus on the two actors establishes a connection between them that outgrows the importance of the sequence. Hearing the conversation solves Gordon's problems.

Brian De Palma's technical devices always serve the moments and the characters they accompany. In *Dressed to Kill*, the slashing of Angie Dickinson's hand with a straight razor is viewed through an assemblage of quick shots taken from different angles. This editing is as sharp as the slashing itself, and the quick shots convey the feeling that the pain is numbed by the unexpectedness of the action. Here, De Palma puts the audience in the same position as the victim.

In *Carrie* and *The Fury*, the main characters have supernatural powers. When their telekinetic juices are in motion, De Palma conveys this by making quick jump shots toward the actors, rather than by tracking in on them. In *Carrie*, when John Travolta and Nancy Allen are about to run over Sissy Spacek with their car, she looks back at them. De Palma presents quick shots that move, each time, closer to Carrie's face, until she provokes the explosion of the car. De Palma used the same effect in *The Fury*, when Amy Irving is suddenly taken over by the force of her powers. The jump cut traveling is what sets apart reality from the supernatural, and serves as the link between normality and the world of telekinesis. De Palma had first used this device in *Sisters*. Near the end of the film, Margot Kidder is kissing William Finley when suddenly, there are quick shots toward their faces. In the last one, Kidder opens her eyes and we know, because of the camera's movement, that we have left Danielle's world and entered Dominique's.

De Palma used the same movement in reverse in *Blow out*. John Travolta is on a bridge recording sounds. Instead of a jump cut traveling toward the actor, De Palma used one traveling away from him to give a wider view of the bridge's surroundings. It gives a feeling of the variety of sounds that Travolta might tap into, and also communicates that the film's plot will contain elements that are less intimate than in De Palma's previous thrillers.

The 360 degree movement of the camera is yet another aspect of Brian De Palma's style that visually develops the feelings of the characters and helps the audience share their emotions.

One of the most moving moments in *Carrie* is the scene where Sissy Spacek dances with William Katt at the prom for the first time. Spacek and Katt are falling in love. They dance close to each other and the camera circles around them. By continuously circling around the actors, who are moving in the opposite direction, De Palma visually recreates the dizziness the characters feel. This technique is repeated in the last scene of *Obsession*. As Genevieve Bujold falls into Cliff Robertson's arms, the camera begins to make full circles around them, conveying the confusion of this intense moment. The circles in both *Carrie* and *Obsession* also symbolize the union that suddenly brings the characters together.

In *The Untouchables*, when the four men are celebrating their first victory around a table, the camera turns around them—but suddenly the movement stops, telling the audience that their friendship won't last. Later in the film, two of the four men are murdered. In *Carrie*, the reason why the circle around Sissy Spacek and William Katt was not discontinued, despite the tragic twist that follows, is that both characters die. The union between them that was suggested by the camera movement also implied that they would have a mutual fate. When William Finley sings his cantata in *Phantom of the Paradise*, the camera circles around him. But the movement is suddenly broken by a short shot of Swan (Paul Williams), who is listening to Finley and planning to steal his music. The broken circle visually announces the singer's disastrous destiny.

In *The Fury*, Brian De Palma uses half circle camera shots of his actors. The camera cuts back and forth from one actor to another in a scene with Kirk

Douglas and his son (Andrew Stevens), and in another sequence with Amy Irving and Carrie Snodgress. The camera travels in half circles because the characters are soon to be separated—Andrew Stevens is taken away from his father by John Cassavetes and Carrie Snodgress dies when she helps Amy Irving escape from the institute. The incomplete movements foreshadow this imminent separation; the half circles implying that the connection between the characters was only temporary.

In *Body Double*, when Craig Wasson seduces Deborah Shelton outside a tunnel after chasing the Indian who stole her purse, the camera makes continuing circles around their embrace. The movement gives a surrealistic dimension to the scene, and also makes the rupture even more powerful when Shelton resists and runs away. The abrupt transition, when De Palma cuts from circular movements to a conventional shot, conveys that the magic of the moment has suddenly been shattered.

The director creates similar feelings in a scene in *Blow Out*. John Travolta has recorded the sound of a gunshot during a car accident; his tape is the only proof that it was a setup. Travolta goes home, listens to the tape, and realizes that it has been erased. He panics, checks out his other tapes, and hears that they've all been magnetized. During this scene, the camera scans the room several times, accomplishing 360 degree shots. It expresses the emotional reaction of the character. He is losing control, and the continuous scanning of the camera visually reveals the confusion he is feeling.

In *Obsession*, the camera pans horizontally, circling over a field that has been transformed into a park where Cliff Robertson has built a memorial to his wife and daughter, and thus telling us that years that have passed since their deaths. This single shot conveys that the park has been the only change in the man's life since the death of his family, and that the loss of his wife and daughter has been the focus of his whole existence. The movement of the camera reveals the loneliness inside the character, just as it revealed John Travolta's panic in *Blow Out*.

Brian De Palma's various visual concepts offer the audience many perspectives from which to evaluate his films' action and characters. *The Untouchables*, for example, opens with a high angle shot from the ceiling above Al Capone (Robert De Niro), who is being shaved in front of a large group of reporters. Nearly every time De Palma films the character of Capone, he chooses to do either a high or a low angle shot of him. This pattern reflects the psychological make-up of Al Capone himself: he is a powerful man (he seems to be dominating in the low angle shots), but he is surely not invicible (the high angle shots create the reverse effect—Capone seems to be vulnerable, as in the opening scene, where his throat is at the mercy of the barber and he is surrounded by journalists badgering him with questions).

De Palma used high angle shots to film the scene in *Carrie* where Sissy Spacek is locked in her praying closet by her mother. The director also puts the camera above John Travolta when he is sitting among his erased tapes in *Blow Out*. In both cases, the camera dominates the characters, and creates the impression that they have become powerless.

In *The Fury*, De Palma combined the high angle shot with a traveling shot. As in the opening scene of *The Untouchables*, the camera slowly moves down toward the central character, Charles Durning. Amy Irving has made Durning's hand bleed by grabbing it while in a trance state. Immediately afterward, Durning has a meeting with his staff of doctors and nurses. The camera is placed above the meeting table, and travels down to end on a close-up of the blood-soaked bandages on Durning's hand. This shot accompanies Durning's warning to his staff that being close to Irving may cause heavy bleeding. It not only illustrates Durning's dialogue, but also it shows how powerless they all are when exposed to Irving's supernatural abilities.

Brian De Palma's direction emphasizes the importance of small details. The audience is intended to share intimate details that relate directly to the characters. At first, these details can seem gratuitous, but their importance always resonates later in the films.

Cliff Robertson, in *Obsession*, sits alone in his hotel room, just after meeting Genevieve Bujold. His back is to the camera, which is placed high above the actor at the end corner of the room. It slowly travels toward his hand, which holds a picture of his dead wife. This long tracking shot, ending on a detail, suggests the dilemma that Cliff Robertson faces. The fact that we see him from the back makes us intruders—this feeling emphasizes the moment. De Palma has neatly informed us that Robertson is torn between the guilt he feels about his wife and the hope that the woman he just met, who looks so much like her, will give him the chance to start over.

In *The Untouchables*, De Palma films what seems to be a gratuitous traveling shot on a matchbox where one of Capone's hitmen has written Sean Connery's address. The importance of this detail only becomes clear at the end, when Eliot Ness finds the matchbox and holds with it the proof that his friend was murdered by Capone's hired killer.

When Margot Kidder, in *Sisters*, makes love to the man she just met on the TV show "Peeping Toms," the camera, by tracking on the scar on Kidder's belly, conveys that the man is in danger. The traveling shot gradually builds up from an erotic start (the couple is kissing on the sofa bed) to a dramatic and fightening vision (Kiddler's robe falls to the side, revealing the mutilation of her body). Here, the camera has taken us from normality toward abnormality, hinting that the horror is yet to come.

By juxtaposing fantasy with reality, De Palma often orchestates his scenes in a unique way. The complexity of his visual elements then justify his characters' behavior, as well as the entanglements of his plots. Craig Wasson, toward the end of *Body Double*, has a claustrophobic attack when the killer pushes him into a freshly dug grave. Wasson is paralyzed with fear and the killer starts to bury him. Wasson feels as powerless, as he did when he played a vampire in his coffin in the film within the film. To explain clearly how and why Wasson is going to take action, De Palma links the current action to the shooting of the vampire movie, and to Wasson's inability to act because of his phobia. The camera retreats, and we are on the set of the vampire movie. Wasson tells the director that he can do it, he can act, because he knows that if he fails this time, he will never be able to get another acting job. He knows that if he doesn't fight his phobia, he will be buried alive by his fear. Wasson climbs back into the coffin, and then De Palma cuts back to Wasson's confrontation with the killer. Wasson takes control and eliminates the killer. The connection between the two scenes visually justifies the dramatic change in Wasson's behavior.

In *Obsession*, Genevieve Bujold, after blackmailing her father, is forced to return to Italy by his partner, John Lithgow, who had set up the kidnappings. Lithgow and Bujold are walking toward the departure gate and Bujold suddenly has a flashback of herself as a little girl being taken to the plane right after her mother died in the car accident. Instead of choosing to have the part played by a young girl, De Palma decided to have Bujold play the role. Bujold is filmed in high angle shot, which makes her look small. She looks so vulnerable that we forgive her for blackmailing her father; we understand that Lithgow had made her believe her father was responsible for her mother's death. The technique of having Bujold play herself as a little girl is what allows us to identify with her character and believe in her sincerity. If the part had been played by a child, the scene would not have worked on such an emotional level; it would have created a rupture between the present time in the film and the flashback.

In *The Fury*, a doctor (Carol Rossen) asks Amy Irving to look at a picture of Andrew Stevens. Irving says that though she's never met him before, she feels that she knows him. Suddenly, Irving has a vision of the brainwashing Stevens endured when he was forced to watch the tape of his father's boat exploding. Irving sees the action as it took place from Stevens' point of view. De Palma cuts back and forth between the vision and the present, where Amy Irving is having a psychic experience. To translate the feeling that Irving has actually become Stevens, he never shows the young man during the flashback, but instead films Irving's reactions. This sophisticated transposition introduces the fact that Irving has the power to see the past, to enter another person's personality, and to feel the events in her vision as if she were living them herself.

The transformation of Jennifer Salt into one of the Siamese twins in *Sisters* is a symbol, as well as a way for De Palma to reveal Margot Kidder's secret. Jennifer Salt "becomes" Dominique and experiences Kidder's psychosis. This device is De Palma's key to avoiding long explanatory speeches. Instead, he prefers clever transpositions of scenes or characters.

The visual conceptions of certain scenes in De Palma's films create a great deal of subtext to the action. For example, in the last sequence of *Carrie*, there is one element that gives away the fact that Amy Irving is dreaming the action—in the background, cars travel backwards. In *Blow Out*, when John Travolta drives into the middle of the Liberty Day Parade, his car crashes into the window of a department store. In the window, there is a mannequin dressed up in costume, with a rope around its neck, standing on a small pillar ready to be hanged. When Travolta runs into the window, it pushes the mannequin off the pillar and the rope slides around its neck. This shot connects to the scene in which Travolta finds a cop friend hanged in a toilet by the wire of his microphone, as well as to the shot focused on the legs of a prostitute being pulled up and strangled in the ladies' room of a train station. The mannequin hanged in the window by John Travolta's accident foreshadows the tragic end of Nancy Allen (she is strangled with a thin rope).

Some elements in De Palma's films are noticable only after a second viewing. For example, De Palma sometimes first introduces characters—who will have major parts later in the story—as extras. In *Sisters*, William Finley is seen among the audience in the TV studio where the game show "Peeping Toms" is being taped. In *The Fury*, a man who jogs behind Amy Irving and Charles Durning as they walk through a park, is later revealed as one of John Cassavetes' hit men. Doctor Elliott, dressed as a woman, stands outside the museum watching Angie Dickinson in *Dressed to Kill*; he can hardly be noticed among the crowd, since the character of Bobbi is not introduced to the action until much later.

Since *Dressed to Kill* centers on a character's split personality, De Palma adjusted his style to the subject by using mirrors in many of the scenes. The mirror symbolizes Michael Caine's dilemma in the movie: he is in conflict with his image of himself. During one of Angie Dickinson's sessions with Caine, her psychiatrist, she asks him why he won't sleep with her. Caine instinctively looks at himself in a large mirror, and answers that he doesn't think she should jeopardize her marriage. Early in the film, De Palma exposes the duality that inhabits Michael Caine. After Angie Dickinson is murdered, Michael Caine comes home and listens to his answering machine messages. On the tape, a detective tells him of the death of his patient and asks him to come over to the precinct. Caine acts surprised when he hears the news, and as he retreats, he bumps against a large mirror. He looks back at his reflection and scares himself. Here again, there is a hint that Caine knows that his image in the mirror is not an honest reflection—knows that he is also Bobbi, a woman trying to come out, and that he is the murderer. Later, Nancy Allen tries to seduce Michael Caine in order to check out his appointment book. When she begins to arouse him, he again suddenly looks at himself in a small mirror on his desk. At this point, Caine might still be trying to convince himself that he is a man, but when Nancy Allen leaves the room, he takes off his tie and glances at his reflection in the mirror, remembering how much he hates being a man. It is then time for him to become Bobbi.

De Palma first used the symbolism of mirrors in *Phantom of the Paradise*. William Finley has been disfigured and can't bear to see his reflection any more. In his case, mirrors remind him of reality. Paul Williams is about to slit his wrists in his bathtub when suddenly his reflection in the bathroom starts to talk to him. Williams wanted to kill himself because he didn't want to grow old. His reflection—the substitute for the devil—offers to let him sign a pact that will assure him everlasting life; only his image in the mirror will become old. The reflection represents the reality of life; looking in the mirror is accepting it. The mirror can't lie, but the mind can to distort the truth and create an image that no longer reflects reality.

Since the beginning of his career, Brian De Palma has not stopped exploring the visual possibilities that moviemaking offers. He has developed his craft as his subjects grew more sophisticated, but he's kept the eye of a director who gives priority to images. Many scenes in his films give primacy to visual concepts, patterns, and cycles. As with his best visual devices, many themes recur in De Palma's work. Voyeurism, sexuality, guilt, and the double all interact with each other. They come together with De Palma's complex images to create a full relationship among visual concepts, characters, their obsessions, and, ultimately, the audience.

VOYEURISM

FIVE

Playboy: No De Palma movie, from *Hi, Mom!*, in 1970, to the present would
seem complete without a telescope. Are you into peeping, or would you
care to advance some cinematic reason for the fact?

Brian De Palma: The exciting sensuous part of the grammar of film is the
point of view shot when the audience sees exactly what the character
sees, unfiltered, uninterpreted. This is unique to filmmaking. The
moviemaking experience is that of being the watcher, and a P.O.V. shot
through a scope turns the audience into the ultimate voyeur. Yeah,
obviously, it has a negative connotation, but it's exciting too. It's also
part of surrealism of movies, of dream imagery, of your unconscious
desires.

—Playboy,
"20 Questions to Brian De Palma" 1983

Peeping Tom. The expression comes from the British legend of Lady
Godiva, who rode naked on her horse because her husband refused to help the
poor. Only one man dared to look at her, and he instantly became blind.
Peeping Tom is also a cult classic thriller made by Michael Powell in 1960,
about a maniac who kills women and, as he murders them, forces them to
look at their own reflections in the distortion mirror he has placed on his
movie camera. The expression "Peeping Tom" applies to voyeurs—to people

92

who like to spy on others' privacy, and to secretly enter their intimate worlds. In his work, Brian De Palma has approached this theme from many angles. He has explored voyeurism, treating it as an overt obsession, or as a wrong-doing with dangerous consequences, or even as a device to correct injustice. At another level, De Palma attempts to place the audience in the position of the voyeur by offering many different points of view on an action. Sometimes, De Palma offers the perspectives of both the peeper and the peeped, allowing us to decide in which position we would rather be. With voyeurism, De Palma points to the essence of why people go to movies. We like to watch—to observe from a neutral point of view. We like to be in the position of looking at someone who doesn't know he is being watched. We like to dominate by being observers. As voyeurs, we can judge, criticize, or laugh at someone without getting involved. Films represent a way for us to act out our inclination to secretly become part of the lives of strangers. Because we know that we're dealing with fiction we feel free to watch and enter into the privacy of the characters. But while watching is not necessarily wrong, it does result in complicity. In De Palma's films the peeper often witnesses a crime, and if he does not act to save the victim, he is as guilty as the perpetrator.

Brian De Palma has consistently explored voyeurism in his films, the same way master directors such as Alfred Hitchcock, and Michelangelo Antonioni with *Blow Up* (1966), have used this theme as the trigger to their plots. De Palma's approach to voyeurism is rather sophisticated in the sense that the technical aspects of his movies are part of the themes themselves. His obsession with the complexity an image can have, necessarily interacts with his characters' obsessions with watching. De Palma's voyeurs are mostly naive but intelligent and sensitive characters (except, perhaps, for the first one of them all—portrayed by Robert De Niro in *Greetings*). The consequences of their voyeurism lead them to become involved with what they see and witness; the films are in fact the stories of their struggles to prove that what they have clandestinely watched has truly happened.

The voyeur is like the audience: they are both at the mercy of their victims. They don't know what they're going to see. As moviegoers, we never know what the director has staged for us to witness. Voyeurism is an adventure, a discovery, an education, and a danger—and we, as well as the characters in De Palma's films, might not be able to handle what we're about to see. . . .

*   *   *

De Palma's first voyeur was Robert De Niro in *Greetings*, whose obsession with peeping constitutes a substitute to active sexuality. In the film, De Niro reads the story of a young man who becomes a peeper because he can't deal with the fact that women reject him. Though there seems to be no such rejection in De Niro's life, he decides instantly to explore voyeurism, and starts to look for someone to watch. De Niro watches a woman (Rutanya Alda) in a bookstore; appropriately, he is spying on her from behind a book display that reminds one of a window frame. The woman, who believes that no one is watching her, steals books. The owner is suspicious and stops the woman on the street. They argue and De Niro becomes involved supporting the woman and finally convincing the owner of the bookstore that she didn't steal anything. By infringing on this woman's privacy, he has been able to protect her. He has gone from the passive act of peeping to an active role. At first, the woman doesn't understand why De Niro has helped her get away with shoplifting. De Niro justifies his action by explaining to her that he loves to watch people in intimate moments. When he saw her stealing the book, she was trying so hard not to be seen that the intensity of the moment totally thrilled him. De Niro, by watching Alda, was at the same time fulfilling his fantasy and protecting her.

But by helping the woman, De Niro has also found a way to carry his experiment in voyeurism even further. He tells Alda that he wants to make an amateur film with her. Both characters are on the street, and while De Niro explains the setup of the film, we can actually see it happening through a nearby window. We see a young woman, in her apartment, whose description and lifestyle coincide with De Niro's story. This visual concept is almost like a split screen—through it, De Palma has found a way to depict De Niro's obsession with voyeurism by making his audience, also, feel like peepers. We listen to De Niro and Alda, and though they're supposed to remain the center of our attention, we can't help looking at the woman by the window. De Palma makes us realize that peeping is a reality in our own lives, and that De Niro's obsession may apply to us as well.

De Niro takes Alda to his apartment to bring to a climax his experiment in peeping. He asks her to strip in front of a camera. The screen is limited by black bars on the sides, to give the impression that Alda is being watched from outside a window. Here again, De Palma transforms us into voyeurs. During this sequence, we never see De Niro; he is only heard giving Alda instructions. He begs her to strip, and to pretend that she doesn't know she is being filmed. (If Alda were to acknowledge the fact that she is being watched, she would then surprise the peeper in an intimate moment, and therefore *she* would assume the power in the situation.) The sequence ends when De Niro enters the room and has sex with Alda while the camera is still rolling. Sex brings De Niro's peeping to a climactic conclusion: he's fulfilled his fantasy by staging it himself, and has succeeded in making it a reality. His plot has worked out perfectly: by spying on the woman and saving her from being arrested, he assured that he would not be rejected by the object of his voyeurism.

After the success of his first adventure in peeping, De Niro decides to follow a beautiful blond woman—from Central Park to the streets and then to a museum. De Niro watches her from outside the building. He is hoping to be able to repeat his experience with Alda with this new prey. A man next to him, played by Allen Garfield, wants to sell him a Super 8 porno film. To get the man off his back, De Niro decides to look at a few frames, even though he is not interested in pornography—to him, it is a primitive form of voyeurism. Garfield tells him: "Look now, no one is watching you!" Garfield is obviously aware that a peeper can become powerless if he is himself observed. De Niro finally pockets the film and gives five dollars to Garfield. Suddenly, De Niro realizes that the blond woman in the museum is gone. Consequently, and ironically, De Niro has no choice but to become a passive voyeur and console himself by watching the Super 8 porno movie.

Voyeurism in *Greetings*, as well as in most of De Palma's films, is a negative trait. At the end of *Greetings*, De Niro is sent to Vietnam. When an American TV reporter interviews him live in action, De Niro, instead of killing a Vietnamese woman on the air, asks her to strip in front of the camera. Though voyeurism is a solitary habit, a peeper often likes to share his obsession to exorcise his guilt. This humorous touch also conveys De Palma's message—that during the Vietnam War, the media transformed Americans into voyeurs, whose passivity made them oblivious to what was really happening.

After his service in Vietnam, Robert De Niro returns to the home of capitalism to make money on voyeurism in *Hi, Mom!*, the sequel to *Greetings*. De Niro discovers a way to profit from his obsession by making a porno movie. He's moved to an apartment in Manhattan that faces a new building, and he has a clear view of four individual flats (the shot of the apartments together is almost like a screen split in four parts). Robert De Niro meets with Allen Garfield, who has become a porno film producer. He is interested in De Niro's idea—to film his four neighbors in their most intimate moments—and gives De Niro enough money to buy a camera. The next sequence takes place in a photo store, and is filmed from the point of view of a woman looking through the eye of a Super 8 movie camera. The salesman explains to her how to use it and shows her all the camera's features (fade in, fade out, zoom, etc). For practice the salesman tells the woman to focus on a customer—Robert De Niro, who has just walked into the store. Ironically, the woman is one of De Niro's four neighbors, and soon to be the object of his voyeurism.

De Niro discovers from his peeping that the woman in the store is married and has children. She spends her energy filming her family and her building, and even begins to interview her neighbors with her new movie camera. But she cannot yet be considered a voyeur. She is only at an experimental stage; she has not yet discovered that she can start filming people who don't know they're being watched.

From his window, De Niro also sees a man who is constantly visited by women. The first time the character appears on the screen, he is taking pictures of one of his lady friends before they start making love. The third apartment is shared by three young women; two obviously have busy social lives, but the third, played by Jennifer Salt, stays home and seems bored and lonely. The last tenant De Niro peeps on is protrayed by Gerrit Graham. He is a militant civil rights activist who paints himself black for an ad campaign.

But all of this material is not exciting enough for De Niro's porno film. He decides to seduce the bored woman and to film himself making love to her, using the automatic timer on his camera. As in *Greetings*, De Niro succeeds at both staging and taking part in a voyeurstic experience. The occurrence of this idea in both films seems to indicate that voyeurs, by watching others, are probably looking for themselves. A peeper releases his own frustrations by observing others and living through his fantasies. By becoming involved with the object of his voyeurism, the peeper completes the full circle of his obsession—he turns the fantasy into reality. De Niro seduces Jennifer Salt, but when the camera starts to film them, it pans in the wrong direction and instead records Gerrit Graham, who is painting his naked body black. De Niro, unaware of the technical problem, delivers the film to the producer; he is fired when Garfield views the film's contents. By getting involved with the object of his voyeurism De Niro had lost control; by becoming an active participant, he had forfeited the manipulative power of the peeper.

Out of frustration, De Niro trades his camera for a television. TV

From right to left, Robert De Niro, Jonathan Warden and Gerrit Graham play three young men in New York looking for ways to beat the draft to Vietnam in *Greetings* (1968).

The peeper, Robert De Niro, and the peeped, Jennifer Salt, end up together in *Hi, Mom!* **(1970).**

**Margot Kidder as Danielle, the sweet, cheerful, op-
timistic and adventuresome twin in** *Sisters* **(1973).**

"Hello? . . . Yes, I want to report
a murder. A man . . . about 25
and black. I *saw* it just now through
my window!" Jennifer Salt in *Sisters*
(1973).

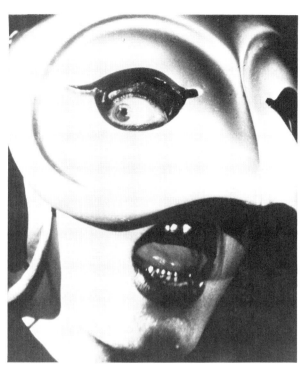

William Finley in *Phantom of the Paradise* (1974), De Palma's underrated rock-horror satire.
TWENTIETH CENTURY FOX

Genevieve Bujold played Cliff Robertson's wife as well as his daughter in *Obsession* (1976). Here with director of photography Vilmos Zsigmond (*left*) and Brian De Palma (*background*).
COLUMBIA PICTURES

**"They're all going to laugh at you!"
Sissy Spacek in** *Carrie* **(1976) should
have listened to her mother's
warnings.**

**Amy Irving will never forget her
prom night.** *Carrie* **(1976).**

Amy Irving and Kirk Douglas in the 'great escape' scene of *The Fury* **(1978).**

Angie Dickinson portrays a sexually frustrated housewife who is brutally murdered after she cheated on her husband in *Dressed to Kill* **(1980).**
FILMWAYS/ORION PICTURES

Brian De Palma and Michael Caine converse between takes on the set of *Dressed to Kill* **(1980).**
FILMWAYS/ORION PICTURES

Tommy Smothers in the dog comedy *Get to Know Your Rabbit* (1972).

WARNER BROTHERS

John Travolta explores a new dimension in peeping and coincidentally becomes the 'ear' witness to a murder in *Blow Out* (1981).

FILMWAYS/ORION PICTURES

John Travolta, Brian De Palma and Nancy Allen (then Mrs. De Palma) during the shooting of *Blow Out* (1981) in Philadelphia.

"I want the world and everything in it." Brian De
Palma directs Al Pacino and Michele Pfeiffer in
Scarface (1983).

Brian De Palma (*right*) **with screenwriter Oliver
Stone** (*center*) **and producer Martin Bregman** (*left*)
on the set of *Scarface* **(1983).**

Craig Wasson and Melanie Griffith in the porn flick within *Body Double* **(1984).**

Kevin Costner (*center right*) **plays Eliot Ness, and forms with Sean Connery, Andy Garcia** (*left*) **and Charles Martin Smith** (*right*) **a gang to fight corruption, illegal liquor and Al Capone during the infamous Chicago prohibition wars in** *The Untouchables* **(1987).**

Robert De Niro reunited with Brian De Palma to play Al Capone in *The Untouchables* (1987) for the first time since *Hi, Mom*! (1970).

From left to right, Sean Penn, Michael J. Fox, and Brian De Palma on location in Thailand, from the Columbia Pictures release *Casualties of War* (1988). Photographer: Roland Neveu.

COLUMBIA PICTURES

ultimately represents programmed voyeurism. From being an active peeper behind a camera, De Niro becomes a passive watcher in front of his TV set.

De Niro ends up living with Jennifer Salt, the object of his voyeurism. Their life becomes a boring routine, at least for De Niro. Suddenly, he, who used to hold the power when he was peeping on Jennifer Salt, is controlled by her. She, as a housewife, has their lifestyle and future all planned out. De Niro can't stand what his existence has become—he's gone from being powerful to being "castrated" by the woman he used to dominate—and he puts dynamite in the laundry room. The building explodes. De Niro has destroyed the object of his voyeurism, and his act has exorcised his obsession, as well as destroyed the woman who reminded him that he had failed as a voyeur.

As in *Greetings*, De Niro ends up being interviewed on television. He makes a statement against violence, though he is responsible himself for an act of destruction. In a way, De Niro is cured of his voyeurism. He has destroyed the building and the people he used to peep on, and has himself become the "watched" by being on television.

In *Body Double*, De Palma explores the theme of voyeurism, by reversing the character developments portrayed in *Greetings* and *Hi, Mom!* The character played by Craig Wasson is a struggling actor, who becomes a voyeur because he has such a hard time being watched. His failing as an actor, as an object of voyeurism encourages him to instead become a passive voyeur. He is easily set up to witness the murder of the woman he peeps on. Although he makes the moral act of reporting the murder, the police are not on Wasson's side: "I got a real problem with you," the Inspector tells Wasson, "I mean, you're my only witness to this murder—and you're a peeper. In my book, that's a sex offender." Craig Wasson is condemned to solve the crime himself because he is a peeper. Craig Wasson's situation indicates that voyeurs are destined to be misunderstood—the logical consequence of their solitary habit of peeping. *Body Double* also confronts the other—possibly dramatic—conquences of voyeurism. (One wonders how the De Niro character in *Greetings* and *Hi, Mom!* might have responded had he witnessed a murder while he was peeping on his neighbors or following strangers.)

Wasson finds his first lead by watching a porno movie, a genre meant for passive voyeurs. It seems as if Wasson has decided to deal only with staged voyeurism, since peeping on his neighbor stripping led to witnessing her murder. With pornography, there is no such risk. But ironically, Wasson connects the masturbation routine of the victim with the one performed by Melanie Griffith in the porn flick. Wasson stars in a porn movie with Griffith in order to solve the mystery. By starring in the film, he has become again the observed. (In the film within the film, he portrays a peeper; his only line of dialogue is: "I like to watch!") Wasson unmasks the murderer because he has placed himself in the vulnerable position of being watched. His voyeurism has only been a projection of his frustration as a failed actor. Ultimately, at the end of the film, after having discovered the dangers of being a peeper, Wasson returns heroically to the front of the cameras, ready to be a confident actor.

In several cases in De Palma's films, voyeurism is used as a device to achieve justice or to fight for a cause. Gerrit Graham, in *Greetings*, portrays a man who wants to prove that John F. Kennedy was assassinated by an army officer, whose name is always censored and replaced by the sound of a "bip." He has a photograph of the assassination, and blows it up to disclose an incriminating silhouette of the officer in the background. His obsession has, in fact, nothing to do with a sense of justice; he just happens to be caught up with discovery he has made through photography, one of the voyeur's most essential tools. Graham is trying to prove that his observation in the photograph is accurate, but the bad quality of the blow up fails to prove his point. Ultimately, Gerrit Graham is shot. He dies because his voyeurism has led him to notice a detail that was a secret. He invaded the privacy of an individual, and he is shot because he knows too much—and more specifically, he's seen too much.

In *Dressed to Kill*, voyeurism becomes the only way for the young man played by Keith Gordon to find out who killed his mother (Angie Dickinson)—and to avenge her death. Convinced that the murderess is one of the patients of his mother's psychiatrist (Michael Caine), he sets up a small movie camera in front of the doctor's office and takes a picture of everyone who comes in and out. Gordon, like Gerrit Graham in *Greetings*, has recorded on film a picture of a guilty party. Nancy Allen, who witnessed the murder, wants to help Keith Gordon in his fight for justice, and decides to seduce Michael Caine in order to look through his appointment book. Gordon is passively posted outside the office with binoculars. Nancy Allen, before she starts to strip in front of the doctor, opens the curtains in the room; Gordon can therefore peep on her to make sure nothing happens to her. Allen is protected by the watcher, the same way the victim in *Body Double* could have been protected by Craig Wasson. But Gordon's peeping on Allen does not have a tragic consequence, because Allen has allowed him to watch.

In *Dressed to Kill*, a blond woman spies on Nancy Allen with binoculars from outside her building. Since we know that the murderess is blond, we're convinced that this woman is the one who slashed Angie Dickinson to death. The peeper is in fact a police officer in charge of protecting Nancy Allen. Peepers in *Dressed to Kill* protect a potential victim—Keith Gordon and the policewoman, thanks to their peeping, are able to save Nancy Allen from being killed by Michael Caine, who is in fact the tranvestic murderer. The peepers in *Dressed to Kill* are like guardian angels. In *Greetings*, De Niro was able to protect Rutanya Alda from being arrested for shoplifting because he had seen her; in that sense De Niro's character is comparable to those in *Dressed to Kill*. The difference between them, however, is that the peepers in *Dressed to Kill* are pure, innocent, and motivated by a sense of justice, whereas De Niro in *Greetings* was motivated by his manipulative schemes.

Blow Out introduces a new dimension in voyeurism: sound. Instead of watching, the peeper listens; instead of filming or photographing, he records. John Travolta plays a sound man who witnesses a car accident. Before the accident, Travolta is established as a peeper—with his microphone, he catches people in private moments. He surprises, for example, a young couple kissing on a bridge. The girl notices Travolta and says: "What is he? A Peeping Tom or something?"

After witnessing the accident, Travolta becomes convinced that it was a setup to kill the Governor inside the vehicle, because on his tape, he hears gunshots before the blow out of the tire. Travolta is the ear witness to the murder the same way Craig Wasson in *Body Double* is the eyewitness to the killing of his neighbor.

John Travolta in *Blow Out* is comparable to Gerrit Graham in *Greetings*. Just as Graham was obsessed with Kennedy's assassination; Travolta is convinced that the sound on his tape is of a gunshot. Graham and Travolta both portray frustrated voyeurs; Graham is unable to get a quality blow up that would prove his point—what he needs, in fact, is the sound of a gunshot, like the one Travolta records in *Blow Out*. Travolta, on the other hand, has the sound but not the picture. He finds out that Nancy Allen—who was in the car with the Governor and whom he had saved from drowning—had a photographer (Dennis Franz) at the scene of the crime. Franz was supposed to catch the Governor and Allen in an intimate moment, in order to blackmail him.

Travolta gets the film, matches it with the sound he recorded, and becomes De Palma's most accomplished voyeur: he's got the sound and the picture!

But just as for Gerrit Graham in *Greetings*, Travolta's discoveries lead to a tragic twist. The evidence is destroyed, and Nancy Allen is murdered. All that Travolta has left of her are his tapes of her screams at the time of her death. Travolta has failed to use his voyeurism to do justice and *Blow Out* ends the way it began—the peeper is left with only a sound, and nothing else to go with it.

The plot of De Palma's comedy *Home Movies* centers, once again, around voyeurism. In this film, De Palma gives humorous treatment to a theme he usually deals with seriously. Consequently, peeping, though explored on different levels, never attains a dramatic climax. The opening sequence introduces the Maestro, played by Kirk Douglas. He has a therapy group in which people are instructed to become the stars of their own lives in order to face the dilemmas of existence. His "star therapy" demands that the participants record their own lives on film. The Maestro tells his students that the camera never lies. A voyeur who peeps on himself is ultimately confronted with reality, and this process should cure the peeper of his frustrations.

The Maestro believes he's found the perfect guinea pig for his experiment in Keith Gordon, an insecure young man. Gordon is desperately trying to get his mother's attention, and in order to win her respect, he decides to help her get grounds for a divorce. Gordon needs to take pictures of his father having sex with his nurses. Unfortunately, on that particular night, there is not much action, and Gordon gets bored until he sees a woman in a nearby apartment walking around half naked. He peeps on her until the Maestro catches him in the act. Kirk Douglas had in fact set Gordon up: he tells him that the woman was a film projected on a screen placed against the window. The Maestro tried to explain to the young man that if he wants to receive the attention he deserves, he should watch himself live rather than peep on others. The Maestro's device to get Keith Gordon to become the subject of his star therapy is similar to the killer's scheme in *Body Double*. Gregg Henry paid a woman to do a masturbation routine that he knew Craig Wasson would be watching; then Wasson became the witness to the murder of Henry's wife. In *Home Movies*, the Maestro tempts Keith Gordon with the image of a woman in her apartment to show him that he needs to turn to star therapy to exorcise his voyeurism.

Gordon agrees to participate, and the first scene he shoots of his own existence is his bedtime, a very private moment. But in the meantime, he has fallen in love with Nancy Allen, his brother's fiancée. Allen had formerly been the star of a peep show, and her husband-to-be is trying to exorcise her desire to constantly expose herself to voyeurism—ironically, by having her watched and followed. Eventually, Allen becomes the object of Gordon's voyeurism; he's ceased to concentrate on watching himself live. He peeps on her through the keyhole of her bedroom and starts following her. Eventually, he saves her from being raped, and here again we see that the peeper often plays the role of a guardian angel. Gordon is able to protect Allen, because he'd been so uneasy with himself that he'd felt the urge to watch someone else. Keith Gordon succeeds where Craig Wasson fails in *Body Double*; he saves the object of his obsession. It is this heroic action that resolves the conflicts in the young man's existence.

Gordon finally decides, after all, to use his movie camera to film his father with one of his nurses. In this case, Gordon's voyeurism becomes a weapon to denounce his father's unfaithfulness. Gordon uses film and voyeurism against his father, taking literally what the Maestro has taught him—that "the camera never lies."

Toward the end of *Home Movies*, Keith Gordon finds himself misunderstood and alone—a common destiny of De Palma's voyeurs. But at the last moment, he bumps into Nancy Allen and she decides to follow him to college. Gordon has at last found a way to be the star of his life, which is to never leave the object of his voyeurism.

Sisters presents two kinds of peepers: a coincidental witness to a murder and a victim who is punished for having been a voyeur. In the opening sequence, a blind woman, played by Margot Kidder, enters a locker room and starts to undress. She doesn't suspect that there is a man in the room watching her. Suddenly, the frame freezes and a keyhole appears on the screen. We realize that we are watching a television game show entitled, most appropriately, "Peeping Toms." It is a kind of Candid Camera–type show. Margot Kidder is in fact not blind; she is an actress/model, whereas the man in the locker room does not know that he is being filmed. He is obviously a voyeur because his decision is not to reveal his presence to the woman. Ironically, he is also himself the victim of voyeurism, since a hidden camera is filming his reaction. The contestants on the show have to guess what the man's reaction is going to be—both players make the wrong choice. De Palma already hints here that peepers are losers; the man in the locker room, himself a voyeur, might also be destined to lose, or maybe even die.

The man is introduced to Margot Kidder after the setup is revealed to him. They flirt with each other. Like De Niro in *Greetings* and *Hi, Mom!* Craig Wasson in *Body Double*, or even Keith Gordon in *Home Movies*, the peeper's ultimate fantasy becomes to make love to the object of his voyeurism. In *Sisters*, this object, Margot Kidder, is seduced by the man she had herself set up to become a voyeur. The next morning, as Kidder murders the man, the room suddenly gets brighter; it is obvious that someone off screen, (De Palma himself?) has pulled up the curtains, inviting all the peepers at their windows to look. In De Palma's first thriller, *Murder a la Mod*, an actress was stabbed in the eyes. In *Sisters*, Margot Kidder is a blind female victim of a man's voyeurism in the opening sequence, and she gets her revenge by stabbing the man in his genitals. She hits the part that led him to become a voyeur. From this example, it seems that De Palma moved from thinking the eyes were to blame to thinking that voyeurism was a sexually motivated act.

Immediately after he's been stabbed, the man instinctively drags himself toward the window. He is himself a voyeur, and therefore he knows that there must be someone out there watching, and that this person might save his life. Actually, the previous night, he had himself watched a woman in her apartment from Kidder's window. Jennifer Salt portrays this woman, a journalist, who, indeed, happens to witness the murder. But, like Craig Wasson in *Body Double*, Jennifer Salt arrives too late to save the victim. Since the police won't believe her, she inquires on her own, and ultimately discovers the mystery, but there are forces at work stronger than her sense of justice, and she is unable to avenge the murdered man's death.

In several of his films, De Palma treats the movie camera as the voyeur. In *Phantom of the Paradise*, Swan (Paul Williams) has cameras everywhere, filming everyone within their own worlds. The camera is the eye through which Swan finds a way to control his people. When Swan is in bed with Jessica Harper, Phantom peeps on them from the bedroom ceiling window, ignoring the fact that Swan can see him on a small TV monitor. Swan is powerful because, thanks to the camera, he is always in the position of watching.

In *The Fury*, the cameras constantly filming inside the Paragon Institute give the evil John Cassavetes the power to control all situations. The cameras allow him to spy on the private moments of the doctors and patients inside the Institute, and what he sees allows him to manipulate these people—gives him the right to decide, for example, whether they should live or die.

Brian De Palma invites his audiences to witness a seduction, a mystery, a murder. *Body Double*—you can't believe everything you see.

The ad campaigns for De Palma's *Dressed to Kill* and *Body Double* emphasized voyeurism; the posters for both films showed a man peeping on a woman. Voyeurism was the hook to get audiences into theaters. But De Palma offers the public more than just the chance to watch and witness the action in his films. He offers an education, by exploring the different levels of voyeurism and its consequences. The lessons are taught through the stories of the peepers in his movies, who inevitably get caught up with their obsessions. Most of them have then to prove that they are more than just passive observers; they have to show that they can take action and eventually, perhaps, become heroic.

Film watching is itself a passive state of voyeurism, and De Palma is certainly trying, through the recurring theme of voyeurism in his films, to sharpen the awareness of the audience. De Palma warns his audience: don't let yourself be manipulated, and if you are, then take action. De Palma's message to us is: don't believe everything you see.

SEXUAL DISTURBANCES

SIX

KATE

Do you find me attractive?

DOCTOR ELLIOTT

Of course!

KATE

Would you want to sleep with me?

DOCTOR ELLIOTT

Yes!

KATE

Then why don't you?

—Angie Dickinson seduces Michael Caine
in *Dressed to Kill*, 1980

DOCTOR ELLIOTT

What sort of man turns you on?

LIZ

Mature, doctorly type . . . like you.

DOCTOR ELLIOTT

Are you sexually attracted to me?

LIZ

Yes, and you?

DOCTOR ELLIOTT

This is not a social visit, is it? You came here to get psychiatric help and my job is to offer you emotional assistance.

LIZ

How about some sexual assistance?

—Nancy Allen seduces Michael Caine
in *Dressed to Kill*, 1980

A few years ago in Minneapolis, a woman set herself on fire to protest pornography. With such extreme feminist reactions to perceive violence against women, it was inevitable that Brian De Palma's vision of sexuality in his films would create an everlasting controversy.

Although his films are not pornographic (De Palma declares: "I don't think my movies have people coming in their seats!"), the themes of prostitution and of the dangerous complacency of rich housewives have given De Palma a bad reputation. Perversely, the more De Palma was assailed, the more he tried to shock those who were trying to censor him.

It is true that De Palma's films contain an overwhelming abundance of sexuality. Of course, one could argue that the director chooses sex as an easy way to hold his audiences' attention and sell his movies. But his approach is more complex, and very seldom gratuitous. De Palma's films contain a lot of sex because they are about sexuality, just as they contain violence because they concern violence. In other words, the director never uses sex or violence, or the two together, simply to create an effect; he uses them to propel his complex stories and to motivate the confused behavior of his characters.

De Palma often presents sexuality as a frightening thing, a sin, a weapon, or even a defense (as when Nancy Allen in *Dressed to Kill* uses her physical appeal to prove herself innocent). Through sex, the characters in De Palma's films reach a point of no return—their sexual impulses often lead to punishment, psychological guilt and harassment, or even death.

In fact, De Palma's cinematic visions of the dark side of sexuality subliminally address our own secret fears. De Palma's exploration of the theme—as it interacts with danger, murder, incest, and the supernatural—speak to the trauma sex is causing in our society (trauma which, tragically, has reached new heights with the current health crisis).

Sexuality in De Palma's films often fills the audience with feelings of discomfort, terror, and disturbing self-consciousness. De Palma treats sex like voyeurism. It, too, can be extremely dangerous and can dramatically alter people's lives.

It is true that the sexual perspective in De Palma's films is cynical, even outrageous at times, and can be viewed as offensive toward women. But De Palma is not attacking women; he is attacking puritanism. He mocks the hypocrisy of a society that has repressed and intellectualized sexuality. By reversing the roles, so that the educated woman becomes the victim and the prostitute becomes the heroine, De Palma challenges our stereotypes.

De Palma's treatment of sexuality is often subtle and complex. In *Obsession*, he explores the legendary and Freudian myth that claims some ambiguous sexual feelings inevitably exist between father and daughter. Though De Palma avoids giving too many details about the relationship that evolves between Genevieve Bujold and Cliff Robertson (it's never clear whether they sleep together), *Obsession* is a story about incest.

When Cliff Robertson's wife and daughter died in a car accident, he lost with them the symbol of his manhood (his wife) and the symbol of his fertility (his daughter). When, years later, Robertson meets a woman he believes is his wife's look-alike, he instantly falls in love with her. By loving a woman who symbolically represents his wife, he's finally found a way to regain his virility.

Genevieve Bujold knows that Robertson is her father. She secretly holds her father responsible for her mother's death, and decides to use his vulnerability to seduce him and to exact her revenge. Bujold plots against her father until she discovers he wasn't to be blamed for the accident. Bujold then decides to kill herself by slitting her wrists; she wants her suicide to be an act of purification in order to exorcise the incestual urges she used to kindle the hatred she felt for her father. The blood of her wounds also suggests that Bujold has had intercourse with Robertson. She has bled. She has become a woman. She must die in the blood that symbolizes her sin.

But Bujold's desperate act doesn't kill her. Instead, she is confronted by her father, who finally realizes that the woman he is holding is truly his daughter. Though their incestuous past can't be erased, Robertson and Bujold forgive each other. Sex is, after all, what revealed to Bujold that her father was innocent, and helped her discover the love her mother probably felt toward him. For her, sex had been a way to manipulate her father, and then became a way for her to understand him. Sexuality in *Obsession* is not as overt as it is in most of De Palma's later films; here he uses it first as a weapon, then as the catalyst that resolves the conflicts between Robertson and Bujold.

Sexuality in *The Fury* is often suggested in scenes of people eating. Amy Irving, for example, never has sex during the course of the story, but is several times seen eating. In one scene she even appears to be a compulsive eater: She and Carrie Snodgress are having ice cream sundaes, and their discussion orbits around sex. Both seem sexually frustrated (Irving is alone and Snodgress hardly ever sees her boyfriend), and food appears to serve as a substitute for sex.

The relationship between Amy Irving and Andrew Stevens in *The Fury* certainly has sexual overtones. They have the same supernatural powers— they were born at the same time and are like psychic twins—copies of one another. Throughout the film, Irving searches for Stevens; she wants to be with a man with whom she feels she has a blood relation. When, at the end of the film she finally finds him, he is dying. She holds him, they look into each other's eyes, and he transmits his powers to her. For them it is the ultimate communion, and the ultimate act of love—of coming together.

Both Irving and Stevens have the power to make people bleed. Irving is afraid of her abilities; she refuses to touch anyone and to let anyone near her. Her caution leaves her few alternatives: if she wants to make love, she'll have to make love with Andrew Stevens, her psychic brother. In fact, her search for him is primarily motivated by her desire for sex.

Stevens is depicted as a modern vampire: he gets his energy by making people bleed. Toward the end of the film Stevens succeeds in making Fiona Lewis bleed to death without even touching her. Through this ultimate "mating" Stevens becomes ultimately powerful.

Amy Irving develops her psychic power in much the same way her young girlfriends develop their sexuality. At first she is afraid of its onset; later she learns to master it. Ultimately she uses it against the evil John Cassavetes.

After Andrew Stevens dies, Cassavetes tries to seduce Irving. He attempts to play a father figure who would also provide her with the affection of a lover. But while he is kissing Irving, blood suddenly starts to pour from his eyes. Irving then, literally, makes him explode.

This orgasmic ending echoes the scene in *Carrie* when Sissy Spacek uses her telekinetic powers to crucify her mother with kitchen knives. The mother's position is the same as Jesus' on the cross. Before she dies, she moans in a sexually explicit way, implying that for her, sex and death are on the same level. This vision, and the image of Irving making Cassavetes explode as a substitute for coming, suggest that according to De Palma, orgasm is synonymous with death for the sexually repressed.

Incest is one of the central themes in *Scarface*. The insane infatuation Al Pacino feels for his sister (Mary Elizabeth Mastrantonio) is one of the factors that will lead to his downfall. For Pacino, his sister symbolizes the stability he'll never find. His feelings toward her develop during the course of the film, and we gradually discover that Al Pacino is in love with his sister. This progression parallels the crisis the hero has to face in his illicit profession. We first notice Pacino's obsession with his sister when Steven Bauer, his right hand man, compliments the young woman's good looks. Pacino loses control. His reaction later becomes actively violent when he catches his sister dancing, flirting and snorting cocaine in a disco. Finally, his feelings are completely exposed when he murders Bauer after realizing he has married Mastrantonio. The young woman confronts her brother with a gun and tells him to face his feelings once and for all. She offers herself to him, knowing that in the end she wants to kill him and possibly also commit suicide. This moment of revelation coincides with a raid on Pacino's house by a gang of elite killers. Mary Elizabeth Mastrantonio is shot, and her sudden death announces the end of her brother's empire.

The incest in *Scarface* is a dramatic and symbolic subplot; it helps to reveal that the Pacino character is a man whose dream—to have the world and everything in it—is as unrealistic as his desire to possess his sister. His repressed sexual feelings—symbolized by his sister—dominated his life. With her death, he became impotent—he lost his power, his protection, his virility, and his life.

In *Carrie*, sexuality—when repressed and distorted—is associated with sin and death. In the first sequence, Carrie (Sissy Spacek) gets her first period in the showers after gym class. Her classmates taunt her for being so frightened by the sight of the blood running between her legs. Later, when she confronts her mother (Piper Laurie), she tells her, "I thought I was dying!"

Carrie is caught between a repressed ultra-religious mother who tells her "men are like sniffing dogs," and classmates who reject her because she is ignorant. Carrie was conceived in spite of her mother's disgust for sex—she was a mistake. Therefore, the girl is predestined to rejection, and to intensely be scared of sexuality.

Carrie's mother is introduced when she drops in on Amy Irving's mother (Priscilla Pointer), who is watching a daytime soap opera on television and having an alcoholic mid-day drink. Laurie launches into a diatribe against sin. During her speech, we overhear the dialogue on TV—a fight between a man and a woman. De Palma tells us that everyday, Americans (and especially housewives), are obsessed with marital and sexual problems—helping to explain Piper Laurie's fanatical attitude toward sex. Laurie believes—from personal experience, we later learn—that sex causes discord between husbands and wives, and ultimately leads to suffering.

Carrie discovers that she's become a woman at the same time she realizes she has supernatural powers. As in *The Fury*, De Palma establishes a link between repressed sexual drive and the supernatural. Carrie's evil powers are substitutes for the sexuality which is absent from her life. But when William Katt asks her to be his date for the prom, Carrie believes it's her chance to finally be accepted by accepting her sexuality. Her mother tries to stop her. When she sees Carrie in her evening dress, she says: "Red, I knew it would be red!" Carrie answers: "Pink, Mama. The dress is pink!" Piper Laurie immediately associates sex with her daughter's dress ("I can see your dirty pillows," she carries on), and with the color of blood. She foresees that her daughter will soon lose her virginity; that she is going to bleed. Carrie's mother then begs her daughter to pray for forgiveness and suggests they burn the dress. She wants to purify her daughter for having what she considers lusty thoughts.

Carrie and William Katt's election as queen and king of the prom has been staged by the girl's worst enemies, portrayed by Nancy Allen and John Travolta. Through them, De Palma brings in another aspect of sex: manipulation. Allen has convinced Travolta to help her humiliate Carrie by giving him oral sex. Travolta agrees to be part of the plot as long as Allen "keeps her tits up" for him. Sex is his reward as much as it is Carrie's punishment.

As planned, the bucket of blood falls on Carrie. Just as in the opening sequence of the film, the girl is humiliated because she is covered with blood. The bucket also hits William Katt, killing him instantly. In Carrie's eyes, Katt has come to represent sexuality as a normal part of life and love. This image is suddenly destroyed, and sex, for her, is again associated with death. With her powers, Carrie kills her classmates and her teachers by setting fire to the building where the prom is taking place. It is her way of avenging their sin against her, but it also offers an apocalyptic vision (which connects with the later disappearance of Carrie's house amid fire and cataclysm).

After turning the prom into a circus of destruction, Carrie returns to her house and takes a bath. Spacek's ritualistic cleansing of the blood seems almost religious. When the girl then turns to her mother to beg for forgiveness and comfort, the disturbed woman recalls the night her husband came home drunk and entered her, conceiving Carrie. Piper Laurie even admits at this point that she loved making love. Sex itself is not her problem. Her trauma comes from the fact that she can't accept her enjoyment of it, and she can't deal with her daughter because she is the fruit of what she considers a sin. Laurie finally stabs Carrie through her ribs—a symbolic reference to the Biblical tale in which Eve is created from Adam's rib. The house is engulfed by evil forces, symbolizing Carrie's punishment for having been seduced by original sin.

Only Amy Irving—who, notably, has sent her boyfriend to the prom with Carrie and remained "pure" herself—survives the bloodbath. But nightmares of Carrie continue to haunt her—another reminder, perhaps, of the dangers of cruelty and of repressed sexuality.

The true antagonist in *Carrie* is the mother. In other De Palma films mothers are also portrayed as intruders—or as scapegoats, but necessarily in direct conflict with the sexuality of the characters. In *Sisters*, Mary Davenport portrays Jennifer Salt's mother. She is opposed to her daughter's career as a journalist, and wonders why Salt can't find a nice man and become a secure housewife. Jennifer Salt is determined to solve the murder she has witnessed and to extract from it a great article that will prove to her mother the value of her ambition. At the end of *Sisters*, Jennifer Salt is back at her parents' house after her terrifying journey. Her experiences seem to support the advice given by her mother, but they have also, perhaps, allowed Salt to prove to herself that she is ready for a more "normal" life with a husband.

Keith Gordon in *Home Movies* portrays a young man frustrated by his mother (Mary Davenport), who only has eyes for his older brother, a latent homosexual. Like Jennifer Salt, Gordon tries to reverse his mother's feelings toward him by performing heroic acts, such as exposing his father's sexual activities with his nurses. Al Pacino's mother in *Scarface* senses her son's attraction for his sister and fears the worst could happen to her daughter. Here again, Pacino carries his infatuation with his sister even further as a reaction to his mother's disapproval.

In *Dressed to Kill*, the mother is used as a scapegoat. When Kate (Angie Dickinson) is in a session with her psychiatrist (Michael Caine), she avoids the subject of her troubled sexuality by complaining about her mother:

DOCTOR ELLIOTT
So, what's happening?
KATE
Nothing much—my mother's driving me crazy as usual.

DOCTOR ELLIOTT

Did you talk to her?

KATE

Yeah, she's hinting around about surprising me for my birthday.

DOCTOR ELLIOTT

She is going to come up from Florida?

KATE

That's the surprise.

DOCTOR ELLIOTT

How do you feel about seeing her?

KATE

Well, I feel I should want to see her. It's been six months since we went down there, but she'll just ruin my birthday and it's my day, not hers.

DOCTOR ELLIOTT

What are your options?

KATE

Well, I could make up an excuse and tell her not to come. No, I can't do that. And let's not forget it's supposed to be a surprise. And anyway, it's not her—I just don't feel up to her or to anything.

DOCTOR ELLIOTT

How are things going with Mike?

KATE

Fine. (*pause*) No they're not fine. What a dumb word that is. He gave me one of his wham/bang specials this morning and I'm mad at him. Isn't that right? Shouldn't I be mad?

Angie Dickinson's mention of her mother leads directly into the heart of her sexual frustrations with Mike, her husband. The mother, in this case, is a way for Dickinson to avoid the painful subject of her relationship with Mike. Dickinson's problems with her mother represent her refusal to resolve her sexual problems.

The maternal relationship that evolves between Nancy Allen and Keith Gordon in *Dressed to Kill* is similar to the one that exists between the same actors in *Home Movies*. Although they have sex in *Home Movies*, Nancy Allen still represents a substitute for Keith Gordon's mother—she gives him the confidence his mother took away by constantly glorifying his older brother. Consequently, their sexual relationship seems almost incestuous (as well as adulterous, considering that the woman is engaged to Gordon's brother). In *Dressed to Kill*, Keith Gordon portrays the same kind of innocent and naive young man. Nancy Allen replaces his dead mother (she tells the young man that she'll be the best cover he ever had), but this time they never sleep together and there is no ambiguity in their relationship. Gordon is in fact asexual; his approach to sexuality is essentially scientific. When Nancy Allen explains to him that Michael Caine was a transsexual, the young man is totally fascinated and declares that this has given him a great idea for a science project: he can build a woman out of his own body!

Nancy Allen and Keith Gordon in *Home Movies* both have at first a fear of sex. For Gordon, sexuality symbolizes the failure of his parents' marriage. He has witnessed his father cheating on his mother, and therefore considers sex immoral. In order to be certain that Nancy Allen is worthy of him, Gerrit Graham (who plays Gordon's brother) puts her through a series of tests to make sure she has renounced her sinful past (she had been a prostitute). After Allen resists the temptations of alcohol, drugs, and junk food, she finds herself having to resist sleeping with a man she just seduced. The man feels insulted and tries to rape her. Allen is saved by Keith Gordon. Ironically, his reward is sex. Gordon and Allen become lovers. What attracts them to each other is that they both have a fear of sexuality. Ultimately, Allen tries to run away from her husband-to-be; she wants to get away from the man who makes her feel that sexuality is a punishable sin, that sex should be feared. The young woman is almost run over by an ambulance; her near-accident completely exorcises her phobia toward sex. By confronting an even greater fear—death—both Allen and Gordon discover that sexuality is, after all, not so terrifying.

In *Dressed to Kill* and *Body Double*, Angie Dickinson and Deborah Shelton, respectively, portray rich, middle-aged, sexually repressed women. Nancy Allen in the first film and Melanie Griffith in the second, however, play women who exploit sexuality for profit. Their objective view of sex saves their lives. Allen and Griffith understand that sex can be manipulative, and therefore they don't make themselves vulnerable, as Dickinson and Shelton's characters do.

In the museum scene in *Dressed to Kill*, Angie Dickinson is surrounded by sexuality. In one corner, a horny young man is constantly trying to kiss his girlfriend while she begs him to look at the pictures, and in another, a man is trying to pick up a woman. It is interesting to notice that in this setup, the men are the aggressors, but when a handsome stranger sits next to Dickinson, she is the one trying to make a move on him. Here again, we see that she is motivated by her frustrations and by her inferiority complex—she is convinced that, unlike the two other women she's just seen, she is incapable of arousing men.

Dickinson's vulnerability is symbolized by her gradual loss of objects. She drops her left glove on the floor—the exposed wedding band flashes a warning. When she throws away her other glove outside the museum, someone—the killer—picks it up. The handsome stranger has the first glove; he actually lures Dickinson into a cab by waving it at her. Later, the woman realizes she forgot her underwear in the cab, which brings her ever closer to danger. Finally, in the elevator, Dickinson remembers she left her wedding ring in the man's apartment. It is this final loss that leads Dickinson directly to her death. By forgetting her ring, she has symbolically lost her marital protection. When she decides, because of the guilt she feels, to go get her ring and resume her role as a housewife, it is too late—she is murdered.

Deborah Shelton in *Body Double* is similar to the Dickinson character on several counts: because of a disinterested husband, she places herself in a vulnerable position by looking for sex outside the marriage; she is a wealthy woman who has time on her hands; she is the aggressor in her extramarital relationship (Shelton buys sexy lingerie and tells her lover she will wear "something special" for their rendezvous). When her lover cancels their date, Shelton's character, by this rejection, doubts her sexual self-worth and it leads her to an anonymous embrace with Craig Wasson, who has been following her. Unlike Dickinson, Shelton resists following through—and she runs away without completing the sexual act. But this doesn't save her. With none-too-subtle symbolism, Shelton is then murdered with a giant drill that the killer holds between his legs. This phallic image of rape and death advances the theory which implies that Shelton and Dickinson both paved the way for their own deaths by losing their self-confidence and by letting their secret desires become synonymous with vulnerability.

Craig Wasson in *Body Double* is a man who feels castrated by his girlfriend, whom he caught sleeping with another man. In the film, he is seeking to restore his virility. At first, his sexuality is in a passive state: he gets off on peeping on Deborah Shelton, his sexy neighbor. Wasson then follows her, and even snatches from a trash can her used underwear, which she has replaced with sexy lingerie.

Wasson regains his potency when he runs after the Indian who snatches Shelton's purse. His heroic decision makes him feel viril again until the pursuit climaxes in a long phallic tunnel. Wasson instantly has a claustrophobic attack, which symbolizes his fear of sex. The tunnel, being the image of an erect penis, suddenly reminds the young man that he feels impotent. Shelton helps Wasson out of the tunnel and arouses him by giving him back confidence and attention. They start making love, but Wasson finds himself feeling impotent again when Shelton interrupts their embrace.

One of the reasons Wasson is determined to solve Shelton's murder is that he feels frustrated for not having accomplished intercourse with her. Ultimately, Wasson is saved from his impotency when he meets Melanie Griffith, the woman who made believe she was Shelton when performing a masturbation routine. Wasson makes love to Griffith, and his virility is at last restored.

Unlike all of his earlier films, *The Untouchables*, contains no passionate scenes—not even any moments of sensuality between Eliot Ness and his wife. Sexuality seems to interest De Palma only when it has negative overtones. The director once declared: "Sex is terrifying!" More than sex itself, it is the fears and the consequences of sex that create the controversy around De Palma's approach to the theme. Ultimately, De Palma is not truly attacking sexual behaviors; he wants to raise the public's consciousness on a theme that is, obviously, still taboo.

Is the violence and the sexual harrassment committed against women in De Palma's films a misogynistic, unrealistic, and outrageous vision? Speculation on De Palma's motives stops where reality takes over: In June of 1986, model Marla Hanson's face was slashed by her ex-landlord, a man who suffered from an inferiority complex and who subconsciously felt rejected by the beautiful woman. A year later, a teenager chased and disarmed a razor-wielding attacker who followed a young female student in Brooklyn and slashed her face. These incidents are reminiscent of the plot of *Dressed to Kill*. Physical harrassment of women is, unfortunately, a syndrome in our society. What De Palma's detractors misjudge as misogyny is in fact a reflection of the social attitude toward women.

GUILT: WHO (REALLY) DUNNIT?

SEVEN

PETER

Mom wouldn't be dead if I had gone with her.

DOCTOR ELLIOTT

I'm Doctor Elliott, your mother's doctor. You shouldn't feel responsible for your mother's death. If you talk about it I may be able to help.

PETER

Do you know who killed her?

DOCTOR ELLIOTT

No.

PETER

Then you can't help!

—Keith Gordon méets Michael Caine
in *Dressed to Kill*, 1980

DETECTIVE MARINO

Hey, you're no witness, you're a suspect! We've got a murder weapon with a nice set of your prints on it!

LIZ

Why would I want to kill that woman?

DETECTIVE MARINO

You were the one with the razor there, you tell me!

—Dennis Franz accuses Nancy Allen
of murdering Angie Dickinson
in *Dressed to Kill*, 1980

Guilt is what creates heroes, according to Brian De Palma. We have seen how voyeurism and sexuality often motivate a character to take action. But these decisions are often also linked to the fear of punishment, or to a feeling of responsibility—in other words, to guilt. In De Palma's films guilt is sometimes reality, and sometimes an obsessive vision in the minds of the characters. In either case, how these characters deal with their guilt determines the outcome of their lives—and of the film.

De Palma's films are the stories of characters struggling to make up their feelings of guilt by accomplishing heroic acts. Some characters succeed in realizing that their guilt is purely psychological, and consequently learn to accept themselves. Others, who have reason to feel guilty, are punished by having to bear the burden of their sins for the rest of their lives—if De Palma allows them to live at all.

Often, abstract feelings of guilt are made concrete when a character is wrongly accused of a crime. But ultimately, whether De Palma treats guilt at a rational level (a character is wrongly accused of a crime), or at a subconscious level (a character feels responsible for someone's tragic fate), it becomes the motivation for action. De Palma studies the human mind at a point where it's left to prove itself—literally or psychologically—guilty or innocent.

Guilt, in any case, puts the characters in a position of vulnerability. The heroes in De Palma's films are at first caricatures of what they will later become; they're antiheroes. They make mistakes, have repressed obsessions, and expose themselves to pain, to abuse, to manipulation, to being made guilty. De Palma's heroes are human, and guilt is the element that humanizes them the most in the audiences' eyes. Guilt, more often than voyeurism and sexuality, is a feeling with which the audiences can easily identify. De Palma uses guilt to elicit response to his plots and involvement with his characters. Since we, the audience, are the ones who will determine the success or failure of his films, Brian De Palma places us in the position of being the judges to the action, hoping that in the end, we will find in favor of the filmmaker.

* * *

Guilt is the main motivating factor that transforms Eliot Ness (Kevin Costner), a simple Federal agent, into a super hero in *The Untouchables*. Ness is a good person in our eyes because he feels guilty, he is human, as opposed to Al Capone (Robert De Niro) who has no remorse and therefore symbolizes evil.

To introduce guilt as the instigator of Ness's actions, De Palma kills what symbolizes innocence. An accomplice of Al Capone's leaves a suitcase in a bar. A little girl thinks that the man has simply forgotten it. She takes it and tries to catch him, and explodes along with the bomb that was inside. Ness feels responsible for the death of the little girl; he feels he should have anticipated the opposition to prohibition.

To emphasize Ness's dilemma, De Palma chose not to show Ness's face in his introductory scene. While Mrs. Ness prepares a snack for her husband in the kitchen, the camera travels to Ness's study, where he has just read the newspaper headlines announcing the bombing. Ness is motionless and obviously moved, but we do not see his face. It is as if the camera—like Ness himself—cannot bear to look him in the eye. The understatement in this scene effectively conveys Ness's deep emotional response, and helps to explain his zealous pursuit of Capone. By personalizing Ness's guilt, especially through his relationship with his daughter, whom he naturally equates with the murdered little girl—De Palma prepares the audience for the extreme lengths Ness will travel to destroy Capone (and, implicitly, exonerate himself).

There is an interesting parallel between a scene in *The Untouchables* and a scene from Steven Spielberg's *Jaws* regarding the establishment of guilt as motivating force. In *Jaws*, Roy Scheider portrays a chief of police who is forced to battle his phobia of water to kill a giant shark. Scheider's guilt stems from the fact that he knew a shark was at large but, because of the Mayor's stubbornness, did not close the beaches. A boy is eaten by the predator and his mother slaps Scheider in public, charging him with responsibility for her son's death. The Mayor tells Scheider the woman is wrong, but Scheider answers: "No, she is right." The guilt that inhabits Scheider ultimately motivates his war against the shark. Guilt transforms him into a hero because he has accepted his responsibility. In *The Untouchables*, Ness arrives at his office and finds himself face to face with the mother of the little girl who has died in the bombing. Instead of making him feel responsible for her daughter's death, she offers Ness her support. The woman doesn't blame him, but Ness still blames himself. Like Scheider's, Ness's feeling of guilt drives his pursuit of the real killer.

These two examples illustrate how, by making their heroes human through their experiences of guilt, both Spielberg and De Palma succeed in evoking audience empathy for their central characters. By being able to identify with the character's feelings, we immediately get on their side and root for them, despite their vulnerability.

Ness reveals his feelings of guilt at several other crucial points in the film: when two of his friends are killed; when he finds a note from his wife that reads "I am proud of you" after he has failed during a raid; and when, while waiting for Capone's accountant, he sees a woman trying to pull a baby carriage up the stairs of the train station where he knows violence is about to break out. This last scene embodies Ness's desire to atone for the pain and the guilt he feels. De Palma has so well set up the sequence by inserting scenes of Ness and his family, and so successfully secured the audience's identification with Ness, that we anticipate his reaction—to help the woman with her baby carriage—though, in retrospect, it strains credulity (the woman takes an inordinate amount of time trying to figure out how she is going to make it up the stairs with her luggage and her carriage).

In the end of *The Untouchables*, Ness finally triumphs against Capone's empire. The success of Ness's challenge totally discharges his feelings of guilt.

De Palma also explores the power of guilt through the character portrayed by John Travolta in *Blow Out*. Travolta isolates himself from the world by being a sound man—he passively listens to life. We soon find out that the cause of this mysterious introversion is guilt.

Before becoming a sound man, Travolta had worked for undercover cops whose job was to expose corruption within the police system. He wired up agents and taped conversations that incriminated corrupt cops. One night a microphone started to burn the chest of an undercover cop. Caught spying, he was hanged with the cable of the microphone. Travolta found his friend, murdered with a device of his invention. Because he felt responsible for his partner's death, Travolta left his former occupation. Paralyzed by guilt, he chose to become passive.

When Travolta relates this story to Nancy Allen, she comments by telling him he shouldn't feel responsible for his friend's death. Travolta replies aggressively: "You tell him that!" Travolta knows that his partner died holding him responsible for the malfunction that blew his cover.

When Travolta discovers that the accident he witnessed was in fact a murder, he's awakened to the possibility of being forgiven for his past mistake. Travolta saves Nancy Allen from drowning; that's his first step toward forgiving himself. By saving her life, Travolta subconsciously makes up for his friend's death. But solving the mystery is a unique opportunity for Travolta to accomplish a heroic and public act that could bury forever the guilt he's felt since the murder of his partner.

In *The Untouchables*, Eliot Ness is given a chance to atone for the little girl's death in the bombing by saving the baby and the mother at the train station. The climax of *Blow Out* completes the same full, but this time tragic, circle. John Travolta finds himself in the same position he was when his partner was killed: he has placed a microphone on Nancy Allen when she delivers the tape of the accident to the man she believes is a journalist—but who is in fact the killer. Allen is also motivated by guilt. She had been with the Governor for blackmail purposes, and she wants to help to expose his murder in order to forgive herself.

Both Travolta and Allen are trapped by, and eventually become the victims of, their guilt. Travolta is unable to save Allen from the killer, and the young woman is murdered. Travolta is condemned to relive the situation which had given birth to his feeling of guilt, and to live out his life feeling responsible for Allen's death.

John Travolta finds only one way to punish himself—to use Nancy Allen's screams at the time of her murder on the soundtrack of the film he is working on. By forcing himself to listen to Nancy Allen's death, Travolta accepts his responsibility (he had immediately left his undercover work after the death of his partner). By facing his guilt, Travolta can at last find redemption and realize that what killed Nancy Allen was his own desire to allow himself a second chance.

Guilt as experienced by the character portrayed by Angie Dickinson in *Dressed to Kill* also engenders punishment. After commiting adultery with the stranger she has picked up in the museum, she discovers papers that indicate he has a venereal disease. Now, even if she lies to her husband about where she spent her afternoon, she is marked by her action. Later, in the elevator, a little girl keeps staring at Dickinson. The child's innocence contrasts with Dickinson's guilt at that moment. Immediately after the girl leaves, Dickinson goes back up to get the ring she has forgotten in the man's apartment—and is brutally murdered. In a way, her last look on innocence foretold her death. Dickinson's feelings of guilt make her vulnerable to the attack by the psychotic murderer.

Guilt in *Dressed to Kill* functions at two other levels as well. Keith Gordon, Angie Dickinson's son, feels guilty about his mother's death. Behind his determination to find her murderer lies his desire to overcome the fact that he feels partly responsible for her death—his mother had asked him to accompany her to the museum, but he preferred to stay home and work on his science project. Gordon's ingenuity and determination succeed in nabbing the killer; the young man is then able to relinquish his feeling of guilt. He also understands that his mother's seduction of her psychiatrist had made her death almost inevitable. Even if he had gone with her to the museum that day, it would only have delayed her tragic fate. But most importantly, Keith Gordon's love for his mother is also what posthumously absolves Angie Dickinson of her sins.

Nancy Allen plays the prostitute who witnesses Dickinson's murder. She sees the killer in a mirror, but when the elevator door closes, she unthinkingly picks up the razor used to slash Dickinson to death—and becomes the number one suspect in the case. Her goal in the film is to prove that she is not guilty—that she didn't commit the murder. Unlike Keith Gordon's, Allen's feeling of guilt isn't only a fabrication of her mind, but her struggle to discover the truth is as determined as the young man's.

She finally realizes that the detective who has accused her of the murder never really suspected her, but wanted her to feel guilty. He knew that her fight for justice would work to his advantage—that Allen would overcome all obstacles and solve the mystery to prove her innocence.

At the end of *Dressed to Kill*, both Gordon and Allen have successfully exorcised their guilt by unmasking the killer. Ironically, the murderer himself is convinced that he is innocent.

Al Pacino in *Scarface* symbolizes immorality. He kills with premeditation, without feeling remorse. But as soon as he lets guilt—in the form of conscience—surface, he must acknowledge all the deeds he had never before considered, and thus becomes vulnerable. Pacino has been assigned to kill an agent, but he refuses to carry out his mission when he realizes the man is with his family. While Pacino has many times made the conscious choice to murder someone, even he cannot unquestioningly carry out the slaughter of innocents. Like Angie Dickinson in *Dressed to Kill*, Pacino is confronted with innocence—symbolized by children—before he is murdered for his sins.

Guilt motivates Cliff Robertson's actions in *Obsession*. He feels responsible for the death of his wife and daughter (he went against their kidnappers' order not to call the police), and his is the story of a man desperately in search of forgiveness. Years later, he meets Genevieve Bujold. Robertson believes she is his wife's look-alike, and to him she represents a unique chance to prove his love and erase his guilt. With her, he intends to start all over, as if the past had never existed.

Bujold and Robertson meet in a church and their discussion symbolically parallels Robertson's feelings. Bujold is an artist working on the restoration of a painting, and she explains to Robertson that several years ago the painting began to peel, revealing another painting underneath. The art scholars found themselves in a dilemma: should they destroy the painting on top to uncover what appeared to be a crude first draft, or should they just restore it and never know what lay underneath. Bujold asks Robertson what his decision would have been. He answers: "Hold on to it [the painting on top], beauty should be protected." "Good," replies the young woman, "that's what the scholars decided." Robertson wants his past—the crude drawing underneath the painting—to be covered up; he wants to forget his guilt. The painting on top symbolizes his wife's look-alike; she is the beauty that he's decided to protect to make up for the sins of his past.

When Robertson realizes that Bujold has been kidnapped under the same circumstances as his wife and daughter, he finds his feeling of guilt tested again. Will he make the same mistake and call the police? Will he hold himself responsible if Bujold is killed? Robertson understands coincidentally that the kidnappings had been plotted by his own partner (John Lithgow), and that Bujold played a part in her own disappearance. Robertson suddenly overcomes the guilt that haunted him. He realizes that he was not responsible for anything—that his partner was guilty. By killing Lithgow, Robertson destroys the man who not only murdered his family, but he also manipulated him, through his mistaken feeling of guilt, to get his money.

Genevieve Bujold, toward the end of the film, feels guilty for having been instrumental in the blackmail of her own father. She tries to commit suicide. Her decision to kill herself appears as an act of cowardice—she refuses to live with the responsibility for what she's done. But Bujold doesn't die, showing that ultimately, it's not up to her to decide whether she is truly guilty. This time, it's up to her father.

Robertson understands that Bujold is his daughter and decides not to kill her. They fall in other's arms, forgiving each other. The guilt they had both felt at one point in their lives was, after all, only a by-product of an obsession.

Amy Irving in *Carrie* feels guilty for having laughed at Sissy Spacek in the gym locker room. Irving can't bear the fact that she participated in the young girl's humiliation. She convinces her boyfriend (William Katt) to take Carrie to the prom instead of herself to compensate for her behavior. This attempt to ease her bad conscience leads directly to the death of William Katt, just as John Travolta's guilt leads to Nancy Allen's death in *Blow Out*. Both Irving and Travolta used another to try to resolve their internal conflict. Because they do not accept the responsibility themselves, their actions have fatal consequences—and give them even more reason to feel guilty.

Guilt in *Carrie* is explored at another level through the character portrayed by Sissy Spacek. She lives in fear of punishment, and this feeling is encouraged by her mother. Carrie struggles in the film to prove to herself and to her mother that sexuality is not a sin and that she should not feel guilty about her decision to enjoy life. Carrie wants to free herself from guilt and when she falls in love with William Katt, her fear is exorcised. What had appeared as a sin is replaced, in her eyes, by the beauty of love.

But Carrie's sudden discovery exposes her to more humiliation by her classmates. Guilt and fear of sin were what had set Carrie up to become an outcast, but tragically, guilt had also been her protection. When she finally released her true self, she made herself vulnerable to her enemies' mockery.

Craig Wasson in *Body Double* combines the roles of the characters played by Keith Gordon and Nancy Allen in *Dressed to Kill*. Like Gordon, Wasson feels responsible for the death of a woman, and like Allen, he is suspected of a crime he hasn't committed. Right after the murder of Deborah Shelton, the detective tells Wasson that *he* is the real reason the woman has been killed. Later, when Wasson calls the detective to tell him he knows who killed Shelton, the detective asks: "Is this a confession?"

The theme of guilt, as explored in *Body Double*, involves both Wasson's fight to prove to the police that he is innocent of the murder of his neighbor, and his struggle to prove to himself that he shouldn't feel responsible for the woman's death.

Craig Wasson achieves his goal when he realizes that he was set up to witness Shelton's murder. Wasson realizes that the event was inevitable, and thereby frees himself of the psychological guilt he had felt. His clean conscience motivates Wasson to become a hero by unmasking the killer; it allows him to discharge the guilt for the crime onto the real murderer.

Brian De Palma takes a comic approach to guilt in *Home Movies* and *Wise Guys*. Nancy Allen, in *Home Movies*, is put through a series of tests by her boyfriend (Gerrit Graham). Graham tells Allen that indulgence in drugs, alcohol, junk food, and sex are punishable sins, and that she has been guilty of all of them in her past. If she wants to marry Graham, she will have to prove to him that she can live a clean existence according to his standards. In a way, Graham expects her to live bearing the guilt of having sinned, and fearing punishment if she should ever transgress again.

The relationship between Allen and Graham is to some extent a caricature of the rapport between Sissy Spacek and her mother (Piper Laurie) in *Carrie*. In both films, the characters who have repressed feelings (Laurie feels guilty for having had sex with her husband, and Gerrit Graham is a latent homosexual) project their guilt onto others, creating scapegoats for their own frustrations. The guilt both Graham and Laurie subconsciously feel motivates them to manipulate innocent and vulnerable prey.

In *Wise Guys*, Joe Piscopo decides to kill himself out of the guilt he feels for having shot his friend and partner—played by Danny DeVito—who was about to gamble away the money they owed the mob. Like Genevieve Bujold in *Obsession*, Piscopo cannot live with his feeling of guilt.

In both situations, the suicide attempts fail. Bujold is saved and forgiven by her father; Piscopo realizes that DeVito is alive and had staged his death in order to fool their enemies. Their feelings of guilt were only temporary, and ultimately served as tests of both Bujold's love for her father, and the friendship between Piscopo and DeVito.

Guilt: 1. The fact or state of having offended. 2. Criminality and consequent liability to punishment. De Palma explores both definitions of guilt in his films. He reveals which of his characters are, ultimately, guilty, and then makes himself the judge of his guilty characters' fates—deciding whether they should live bearing the consequences of their actions, be forgiven, or be eliminated.

Guilt, as depicted in De Palma's films, is often the product of voyeurism and repressed or perverted sexuality. It relates to one of the oldest themes in the world—judged guilty by God, Adam and Eve were cast out of Paradise.

De Palma's heroes are very seldom innocent, but they are often liberated from their feelings of guilt by performing redemptive acts, and by accepting the fact that they're only human and can make mistakes. De Palma also shows that guilt can, sometimes, be a healthy emotion—without it, one can kill and destroy others without remorse.

Yet guilt, rather than motivating heroic action, can instead feed upon itself and engender something even more extreme: the split personality. In the case of Margot Kidder in *Sisters*, for example, her feeling of guilt for the death of her Siamese twin is so great that it reincarnates her sister's personality. Guilt is one aspect that nurtures the death-ridden syndrome of the double.

EIGHT

Int: Police Station

LIZ

Thank God! What was wrong with that guy anyway?

DOCTOR LEVY

He was a transsexual about to make the final step but his male side couldn't let him do it.

DETECTIVE MARINO

Male side?

DOCTOR LEVY

There was Doctor Elliott and there was Bobbi. Bobbi came to me to get psychiatrist's approval for a sex reassignment operation. I thought he was unstable and Elliott confirmed my diagnosis. Opposite sexes inhabiting the same body. The sex change operation was to resolve the conflict. But as much as Bobbi tried to get it, Elliott blocked it. So Bobbi got even.

DETECTIVE MARINO

By killing Mrs. Miller?

DOCTOR LEVY

Yes. She aroused Elliott just like you did, Miss Blake.

LIZ

You mean when Elliott got turned on, Bobbi took over?

141

DOCTOR LEVY

Yes. It was like Bobbi's red alert. Elliott's penis became erect and Bobbi took control—killing anyone that made Elliott masculinely sexual. When Elliott came to my office, it was the first time I saw Bobbi's masculine self. When Elliott told me he thought Bobbi had killed Mrs. Miller, he was confessing himself . . .

> —Nancy Allen, Dennis Franz and David Margulies
> discuss Michael Caine's split personality
> syndrome in *Dressed to Kill* (1980)

All the themes explored so far in Brian De Palma's films are reflections of the characters' repressed impulses. To free themselves of these impulses, the characters have two possibilities. They can take action and live out, accept, or overcome their hidden desires. Or they can create a double, who will accomplish what the primary personality cannot accept or do. The split personality gives birth to a scapegoat who takes over responsibility for all that is evil and destructive.

The split personality, as depicted in De Palma's films, exhibits different levels of pathology. The genesis of the theme is found in *Hi, Mom!*, where De Palma uses a variation on the split personality to make a point about racism in America. He uses an identical device to raise the same issue later, in *Home Movies*. De Palma made the split personality the central theme of *Sisters*, *Dressed to Kill*, and *Body Double*. In these films, De Palma explores the most dangerous and tragic ramifications of creating a double at a conscious or subconscious level.

The theme of the split personality also recurs incidentally in several other De Palma films. The director chose to dwell upon this theme to point out that one of man's greatest challenges in life is to create an identity for himself. We all have secret dreams and hidden monsters, and these feelings often interact with our true selves when reality suddenly becomes unbearable or unsatisfactory. In the extreme, these repressed feelings can subconsciously create a new personality that doesn't belong in the real world—but will do anything to remain there . . .

In *Hi, Mom!*, the beginnings of De Palma's interest in the split personality complex are quite apparent, particularly in the sequence entitled "Be Black, Baby!" After failing as a Peeping Tom, Robert De Niro joins a group that advocates civil rights for black people. The group organizes a seminar to help white people experience what it's like to be black in America.

The sequence is filmed in black and white and set in a warehouse. A group of white people pretend to be black—they "become" black, psychologically and physically (they paint their faces black). The experiment turns violent when the real group of black people starts to mistreat the guinea pigs. Through their role-playing, the white people are suddenly exposed to the violence and discrimination black people suffer every day of their lives.

Robert De Niro, who works with the group of black people who are now acting as if they were white, arrives in the middle of the confusion disguised as a cop. Becoming a fictitious policeman gives De Niro the power he had lost as a peeper. Instead of helping the guinea pigs, De Niro turns against them and treats them as if he were a racist and they were black. Fortunately, the white people suddenly realize that all of this was part of the experiment, and they're released without further abuse.

The "Be Black, Baby!" sequence in *Hi, Mom!*, is a clever way for De Palma to denounce discrimination against the black community with a good dose of satire, but it also introduces the dangers of the split personality. The white people in *Hi, Mom!* come out of the experiment traumatized. They have learned that acting as someone else, splitting their personalities, can lead to a dangerous point of no return where the fictitious self suddenly takes over and eliminates the credibility of one's true personality. In this case, people made a conscious choice to act out false roles, and learned something valuable from their experiences. In his following films, De Palma took his theory further by exploring the causes and effects of the split personality when it is a subconscious choice and a reflection of psychotic behavior.

In *Sisters* there are, in effect, two women with distinct personalities inside the character played by Margot Kidder. Kidder plays Danielle, an attractive and apparently self-confident young woman, who is in fact dominated by the tyrannical personality of Dominique, her dead Siamese twin. The operation that separated the sisters—and killed Dominique—had been performed by Doctor Emil Breton (William Finley), Danielle's lover. Finley is the true cause of Kidder's split personality. By falling in love with Danielle, he suddenly made the pair incompatible, and Dominique's death was a sad consequence of their relationship. Danielle is compelled to reinvent her sister in her mind and then attributes her own murderous impulses to Dominique. To Danielle, any men who arouse her remind her of Breton, Dominique's murderer. Since she believes her sister is still alive, she instantly eliminates the men who, like Breton, threaten to come between them.

Through murder, Kidder finds a way to exorcise the psychotic personality of Dominique. The double she's created in her mind is a scapegoat who expresses the trauma of her existence. Danielle is trapped in a vicious circle: when Dominique was still alive, Danielle couldn't have a relationship with Breton. Now that Dominique is dead, Danielle feels that Breton murdered her, and she cannot accept his love. Danielle breaks out of her entrapment by killing Breton. This act cures her split personality syndrome—through it, she puts her sister's ghost to rest, and makes peace with her own tormented self. At the end of *Sisters*, Margot Kidder has recovered from her psychosis, and is able to admit that her sister died two years before.

The theme of the double in *Sisters* is more than a simple plot line. It is a device De Palma uses to manipulate the audience into believing that Dominique is, in fact, still alive. We as the audience, experience Kidder's split personality subconsciously since, like her, we believe that Dominique is the killer.

Like Margot Kidder in *Sisters*, Michael Caine in *Dressed to Kill* subconsciously creates an internal double who is evil and dominant. Both Caine and Kidder establish dialogues with their doubles, and both argue with the personalities they have created. Dominique is furious that Danielle brought a man back home on their birthday. Bobbi—the alter ego of Doctor Elliott (Caine)—leaves threatening messages on Elliott's answering machine. Obviously, their split personalities express their deep inner struggles.

In *Dressed to Kill*, De Palma explores the themes of both sexuality and split personality by creating a character (Michael Caine) whose double is a woman. Caine externalizes his split personality by sometimes dressing as a woman. His disguise is a reflection of his internal disturbances. Since he has the option, through a sex change operation, of becoming a woman forever, his two personalities are struggling for ultimate possession of his body. Bobbi is a woman trapped inside a man's body; she has no choice but to kill anyone who seduces Elliott's masculinity. The problem for Caine is that Bobbi has, in effect, taken on a life of her own, and to her, Doctor Elliott is an antagonist who must be eliminated. Elliott's two personalities cannot coexist, and are intent upon destroying one another.

Danielle, at the end of *Sisters*, resolves her internal conflict by eliminating the man who had caused it. Doctor Elliott, at the end of *Dressed to Kill*, is arrested, but he is left with the conviction that Bobbi is still out to destroy in order to become real. He may never resolve his split personality, because the cause of his conflict lies within himself.

Nancy Allen, in *Home Movies*, is torn between her desire to marry Gerrit

Graham and become a faithful housewife, and her subconscious desire to give in to sexual promiscuity. Graham has decided to train Allen in respectability. In fact, his effort to help her change personalities allows him to avoid dealing with his own two-sided internal existence: part of him wants to be heterosexual, and another part is attracted to young men. By forcing Nancy Allen to see how "evil" she is, Graham can ignore his own insecurities—by making her self-conscious of her impulses, he can deny ever having had his own "unacceptable" urges.

Allen's split personality is born of her repression of her true desires. These desires are projected onto a second personality, who constantly tries to seduce her into returning to her previous wild lifestyle. Allen's double takes the form of a stuffed rabbit named Bunny (she used to strip on stage with it, and it therefore symbolizes her past), whom she believes is real. Bunny is almost a satirical version of Bobbi, the woman inside Doctor Elliott in *Dressed to Kill*: Bunny, like Bobbi, is trying to destroy Allen's present personality.

At the end of *Home Movies*, Allen lets Bunny completely take over and the experience helps her discover who she really is. By acknowledging her repressed desires, Allen decides for herself to get rid of them, whereas before she had been forced to conceal them. Allen understands that Graham was as bad as Bunny, and as she decides to take charge of her own life, she eliminates both opposing forces from her life. The only one who is still in danger, in the end, is Gerrit Graham, because he hasn't yet acknowledged his own internal conflict.

In *Body Double*, Craig Wasson's double identity is a conscious way for him to avoid reality. Wasson has apparently become an actor because he is haunted by fears and repressed feelings, especially about his childhood. Acting—like split personality—allows him to escape from himself by taking on the identities of fictitious characters. Then Wasson finds out that his girlfriend has cheated on him and that he's been fired from the vampire film he was working on. Suddenly, he is vulnerable in both his worlds—in his real life and in his life as an actor playing other people. Ultimately, Wasson comes out of this trap by solving the murder of his neighbor. He discovers the heroic side of his personality, and this discovery suddenly resolves the conflicts in his life and in his acting career.

At the end of *Body Double*, Wasson returns to acting, but this time, not to conceal, forget, or cover up for the sad reality of his existence. He goes back in front of the cameras knowing that he is a hero on the screen as well as in real life, and that he won't be afraid to switch back to reality when the director yells "Cut!"

The theme of the double operates on an external level through the characters played by Gregg Henry and Melanie Griffith in *Body Double*. Henry is the murderer who chooses to disguise himself as an Indian to accomplish his crime. His stratagem is comparable to Keith Gordon's in *Home Movies*: In order to catch his father committing adultery and help his mother's divorce case, Gordon paints his face black (he is actually at first arrested by a racist cop and suffers discrimination, like the group of white people in *Hi, Mom!*). Both Henry and Gordon use disguise to protect themselves from being accused of their actions, and to avoid confronting the victims—Gordon's father will believe he's been betrayed by a black man and Deborah Shelton will die convinced that she was murdered by an Indian.

At the end of *Body Double*, Wasson literally unmasks the killer and discovers that the Indian was in fact Gregg Henry. By forcing Henry to reveal himself, Wasson eliminates his power. Henry had the force to kill because he knew he was protected by his disguise. As himself, and without his double, he becomes impotent and vulnerable. Henry is attacked by his own dog, and they both fall to their deaths in a canal. The dog's reaction toward his own master symbolizes the fact that Gregg Henry has truly lost all identity.

A "body double," in the film jargon, is an anonymous person who replaces an actor in certain scenes that the actor can't or won't perform, such as stunt scenes or sexually explicit scenes. *Body Double* is a takeoff on this practice. Gregg Henry hires Melanie Griffith, a porn queen, to perform a masturbation routine posing as his wife—thereby aiding his murder plot. The use of the double, in this case, becomes as manipulative as the killer's disguise. By using the technique of the body double as the frame for his film's plot, De Palma acknowledges that a director is able to use the double to trick his audience—as De Palma himself often has.

For example, in *Dressed to Kill* Nancy Allen knows that the blond who killed Angie Dickinson is after her. But she later finds out that the undercover policewoman in charge of her protection was also blond, and that she had mistaken her for the killer. De Palma purposely creates a look-alike of the killer so that we will not suspect that Michael Caine is the murderer. There is even a split screen scene that simultaneously presents both the blond (she is in fact the policewoman, but we think she is the murderer) and Michael Caine. Naturally we assume that Caine and the killer are two different people. It is Bobbi's look-alike who shoots Michael Caine at the end of *Dressed to Kill*, saving Nancy Allen from being slashed to death. This is a rare situation in De Palma's exploration of the theme—the double is seldom responsible for a good deed.

In *Obsession*, Genevieve Bujold becomes the psychological substitute for Cliff Robertson's dead wife. In fact, the substitution is external as well as internal: Bujold looks like Robertson's wife, and her resemblance allows Robertson to subconsciously replace one woman with another. Bujold becomes the copy, the double for Robertson's wife, as if she had returned from the dead to give him a second chance to prove his love.

One scene in *Obsession* effectively illustrates the theme of the double, and explains the way Cliff Robertson recreates the image of his wife through Genevieve Bujold. Bujold tells Robertson the legend of Dante, the fourteenth-century Italian poet, and Beatrice, the young woman he loved:

> You know, as a child, I used to go to the church where Dante came to watch Beatrice. Beatrice, *la bella donna*, would sit here with her father and over there, the young Dante, twenty-three years old, would stand and watch Beatrice. Here, in between, sat the Lady that Dante pretended to love so that Beatrice would not be embarrassed by his continuing games . . . You still love Elizabeth, don't you? That's why you want me.

The legend is about substitution. Bujold knows that Robertson is only obsessed with her because he hopes he can convince himself that she is Elizabeth. He loves Bujold because he loved his wife so much, and she is so much like her. Through the legend, Bujold tries to tell Robertson that by interchanging one woman for another, he is fooling himself. While listening to the tale, Robertson at first thinks that he stands for the father; Bujold immediately corrects him and tells him that he is like Dante. Elizabeth, is Beatrice, of course, and Genevieve Bujold is the young lady. But in reality, Elizabeth—like the legendary Beatrice—has become a ghost, so Robertson must force himself to fall in love with her substitute—her double.

All conflicts are resolved in the last sequence of *Obsession*. Cliff Robertson, by realizing that Bujold is his daughter, accepts that he will never be able to replace his wife, and Genevieve Bujold, by understanding that her father loved his family and had only been set up, is ready to be herself. Bujold herself had been set up by John Lithgow to play the part of the double, just as Melanie Griffith in *Body Double* had been paid to pretend she was Deborah

Shelton. At the end of *Obsession*, both Robertson and Bujold have eliminated the double, the substitute that nearly led to their deaths.

In *Phantom of the Paradise*, *The Fury*, and *Blow Out*, the theme of the double recurs. But rather than a central element, it is an incidental link within the stories, contributing, along with other themes, to the development of the plots.

William Finley, in *Phantom of the Paradise*, is forced to renounce his true personality as a consequence of the accident that disfigured him. To cover up his real self, he is forced to become a ghost, a phantom in disguise. Prior to his accident, Finley had disguised himself as a woman in order to meet Swan, the producer who had stolen his music. Once his true identity was exposed, he was thrown out. It seems that Finley, as himself, is always rejected. He only takes control when he is in disguise—when he pretends to be someone else. As a woman, he could manipulate Swan; as the Phantom, he can take his revenge on the producer. At the end of the film, Finley is recognized for who he really is, and dies. The double was his cover, and the thing that protected him from the real world. But the disguise was only temporary and illusory— acting as someone else didn't solve Finley's problems, just as it didn't help Michael Caine resolve his internal conflicts.

William Finley has also lost his voice in the accident. Through Jessica Harper, the woman he loves, he finds a way to recover some of his talent by having her sing his opera. She is the substitute who helps Finley reconstitute his lost self. The danger that constantly threatens Jessica Harper because of her involvement with the evil Swan, therefore, also threatens Finley.

At the end of *Phantom*, Swan is marrying Jessica Harper. He is wearing a mask. William Finley has sabotaged the videotapes that kept Swan young, and he unmasks the producer in front of the audience. Suddenly, Swan's true identity as an old man is revealed; he had also gone through life pretending to be someone else. Finley and Swan die—their inability to live as themselves ultimately leads to their deaths.

Amy Irving and Andrew Stevens in *The Fury* are doubles. They are like twins, born at the same time and sharing the same supernatural powers. Amy Irving declares that she has always felt Stevens's presence, even though they have never met. For Irving, the only way to accept the fact that she is different (she considers herself a freak, just as the Siamese twins do in *Sisters*) is to find her double. Irving believes that meeting someone with powers identical to hers will help her validate her personality.

The conflict between the doubles in *The Fury* is generated by the character played by John Cassavetes, who wants to use Andrew Stevens's supernatural forces for political blackmail between nations. In order to have total control over Stevens, Cassavetes makes him believe that his father (Kirk Douglas) has died in a boat accident; his intention is to brainwash Stevens into believing that he has become the substitute, the double, the equivalent to his father.

When Amy Irving finally finds Stevens, her double is suddenly convinced that she has come to replace him. Irving had thought all along that they were compatible; Stevens just thinks that they are interchangeable, and that the similarities between them make him useless and replaceable. Stevens is convinced that two copies of the same human being cannot cohabitate.

Stevens finds deliverance in self-destruction. Before he dies, he transmits all his power to Irving. With her powers doubled by her double's, Irving is able to destroy John Cassavetes, who symbolized that which kept the twins apart. By killing Cassavetes, the young woman avenges her double. This act marks a turning point for Irving. Her search for her double ultimately taught her to accept herself. Stevens's death has exorcised her need to find an identity through someone else—who was, after all, only an image of herself.

One of the subplots in *Blow Out* again deals with the extermination of the double. Nancy Allen has witnessed the murder of a Governor and the man who masterminded the plot needs to eliminate her. He decides at first to kill two women who look exactly like Nancy Allen so that the police will believe they are dealing with a psychotic killer obsessed with the image of a certain woman, rather than the man connected to the murder of the Governor. In *Blow Out*, both the real character and her unwitting doubles are in danger. De Palma implies that the creation of a double, intentional or not, almost inevitably leads to death.

De Palma's films remind us that we are living in a society of illusion, of doubles, of clones. We all try to lie to ourselves about who we truly are. The cinema of De Palma is a warning against the consequences of self-deception. It is a call for the audience to realize how easy it is to be manipulated. De Palma's vision of society is dark, but his solutions are often more optimistic than his setups. Ultimately, the director's message is that accepting our shortcomings eliminates our need to create doubles or a false selves to embody "unacceptable" traits—and that this is the key to survival.

EPILOGUE

This book is the result of my obsession with Brian De Palma's work. The first time I saw *Dressed to Kill*, during the opening shower scene, I watched Angie Dickinson give herself pleasure and then suffer rape, and I thought, well, we're hardly five minutes into this film and I'm already overwhelmed with sensuality, suspense, and violence. I don't know what to expect next. De Palma's visual concepts, the way the camera revealed the feelings of the characters while at the same time controlled mine, so impressed me, that the memory of discovering *Dressed to Kill* can hardly be translated into words.

Writing a book on film represents a tremendous challenge because the author has to put into words what is accomplished in images. I wish this book could be accompanied with a videotape to illustrate my points, but since that isn't possible, I sincerely hope I've proved that Brian De Palma deserves more notice than he's received so far. I will feel that this book is an accomplishment if whoever reads it wants to see De Palma's films for the first time, or reconsider and view them again, either to confirm the accuracy of my study or to challenge my ideas with different theories.

Initially I thought the ideal situation for me would have been to have with Brian De Palma a long interview like the one Truffaut had with Hitchcock. This didn't happen for various reasons. First, I'm not Truffaut and second, De Palma hasn't made as many films as Hitchcock had when he permitted

Truffaut to bombard him with questions. (I know that some will advance that as much as I'm not Truffaut, De Palma is not and never will be in league with Hitchcock!)

Regardless of these first two impediments, I tried to pursue the interview. The first time I met Brian De Palma, I asked him for his phone number, which he had to repeat to me at least three times because I was so nervous. I phoned and I'm still waiting for a callback.

Next I saw him at a party for *Body Double*. I approached him with my project and asked if I could have a chance to interview him. He replied, "Look, let me open that movie first!" and walked away. Well, *Body Double* opened and closed in almost the same week and still De Palma didn't return my calls.

Once I waited outside his office in New York for three hours, hoping I would be able to approach him, that he would spontaneously say *yes*, and that the next thing I'd know, I'd be on the *Today Show*. But as I waited I became aware that a man was peeping at me from another apartment. When he became an active instead of a passive peeper, I knew it was time to make a fast exit.

Finally an opportunity came my way and I interviewed Brian De Palma. It was then that I realized it wouldn't work. After so many battles with the press his defenses were up, and even though he was talking to someone who was genuinely interested in his work—he was, after all, intentionally . . . boring! I gave up my idea to conduct an extensive meeting with him for my book and decided to stick to watching his films repeatedly. In fact, better than an interview, his films reveal all that's important to know about his art and about the career of a director who feels he has been hurt, betrayed, misunderstood, underestimated, and yet who still thinks he is the top.

Oliver Stone once told me that there were three things that had kept him going while struggling to become a filmmaker: hate, rejection, and failure. In that respect, De Palma is probably grateful to his enemies. He may be more in debt to them than he is to his supporters . . . like me. As De Palma declared, the ultimate judge over his films will hardly be the audience or even the critics, but time. With *The De Palma Cut*, I hope to have anticipated the answer. However, if some think I am wrong, I'll simply say what De Palma would say, "The critics are wrong, the public is wrong, and *I am right!*"

—Laurent Bouzereau
New York, 1988

LAST SCENE

Free at last, Doctor Robert Elliott settled on a bench in the most deserted area of Central Park. He stretched his legs and breathed in the chilly but bright fall day. Those few years at Bellevue had set him straight. He nodded in agreement with himself, the woman inside him didn't exist anymore. He nodded again and spoke out loud, "Bobbi is dead."

"Bobbi is dead" assertively filled the earphones a young, dark, handsome soundman wore in the distance. He shifted his microphone more directly toward the man on the bench, but he noticed the man watched his every move, so he faded out.

Doctor Elliott discovered a mint in the pocket of his coat and popped it into his mouth. A piece of hair stuck to the candy tickled his tongue. He spat it out—it had looked old enough to vote anyway—and watched it land at the feet of what turned out to be a leggy brunette.

She sat down next to Elliott. An older woman, but still attractive, she wore a beige cape and the more she played with her mane of hair, twisting it into a temporary bun and letting it fall back around her shoulders, the more attractive she became.

"My name is Danielle."

Elliott forced a smile in acknowledgement, but something troubled him. He thought he only had a straight razor in the pocket of his pants.

"I'm waiting for my sister. Her name is Dominique."

Elliott forced another smile to cloud over his growing concern.

"Today is our birthday." She twirled her hair once more, and when she winked at the man he knew he had been wrong. Bobbi was not dead. Despite his frenzy, he noticed as the woman reached for her handbag that her facial features seemed to change. When she spoke, she did not seem to be speaking to him.

"Don't you think he looks an awful lot like Emil Breton, Dominique?" Danielle asked out loud.

Elliott extracted the straight razor at the same time the woman pulled out a kitchen knife. The steel surfaces glinted blindingly in the long rays of the setting sun.

"Happy birthday, Dominique and Danielle," Bobbi said, pulling the razor across the woman's throat, but not in time to prevent Dominique from saying, "Farewell, Doctor." Her stroke—her last—relieved Elliott of his congenital burden.

The whine of a Super 8 camera in the distance captured the scene.

SHORT FILMS

Icarus (1960)

660214, *The Story of an IBM Card* (1961)

Woton's Wake (1962). Starring William Finley; distributed by Canyon Cinema; 1963 Rosenthal Foundation Award for best film directed by a filmmaker under twenty-five.

Jennifer (1964). Screenplay by Bruce Rubin; starring Jennifer Salt and Scott Ghamon.

Mod (1964). Documentary on English pop music groups.

Bridge That Gap (1965). Documentary sponsored by the N.A.A.C.P. (The National Association for the Advancement of Colored People).

Show Me A Strong Town And I'll Show You A Strong Bank (1966). Documentary sponsored by the U.S. Treasury Department.

The Responsive Eye (1966). Documentary on the Op Art exhibit at the Museum of Modern Art in New York City; distributed by Pathe Contemporary.

MUSIC VIDEO:

Dancing in the Dark (1984). Song by Bruce Springsteen, produced by Columbia Records.

FEATURE FILMS:

THE WEDDING PARTY (Shot in 1964–1966, released in 1969)
Directed by Brian De Palma, Wilford Leach and Cynthia Munroe.
Screenplay: Brian De Palma, Wilford Leach and Cynthia Munroe.
Producers: Brian De Palma, Wilford Leach and Cynthia Munroe. *Director of Photography*: Peter Powell. *Editor*: Brian De Palma. *Music*: John Herbert McDowell. *Sound*: Henry Felt, Betsy Powell and Jim Swan. *Mixing*: Jim Townsend. *Costumes*: Ellen Rand. An Ondine Production. Released by AJAY (Arnold Jacobs) Films.
Black and white. Running time: 90 minutes. Shot on Shelter Island, New York and in Pennsylvania.

Starring: Jill Clayburgh (Josephine Fish), Charles Pfluger (Charlie), Robert De Nero [*sic*] (Cecil), Jennifer Salt (Phoebe), William Finley (Alistair), Valda Setterfield (Mrs. Fish), Raymond McNally (Mr. Fish), John Braswell (Reverend Oldfield), Judy Thomas (Celeste, the Organist), Sue Ann Converse (Nanny), John Quinn (Baker), Richard Kollmar Jr. (Jean Claude, the Hindu/ Klaus), Helmut Pfluger (Charlie's father).

MURDER A LA MOD (1968)
Directed by Brian De Palma
Screenplay: Brian De Palma. *Producer*: Ken Burrows. *Director of Photography*: Bruce Torbet. *Editor*: Brian De Palma. *Music*: John Herbert McDowell. *Song*: "Murder a la Mod," written and performed by William Finley. *Sound*: Robert Fiore. *Production Managers*: Riva Freifeld and Beth Hertig. *Credit design*: Dyn Productions
Color. Running Time: 80 minutes. Shot in New York.

Starring: Margo Norton (Karen), Andra Akers (Tracy), Jared Martin (Christopher), William Finley (Otto), Ken Burrows (Wiley), Lorenzo Catlett (Policeman), Jennifer Salt (First actress), Laura Rubin (Second actress), Melanie Mander (Mannequin), Laura Stevenson (Girl in the shop).

GREETINGS (1968)
Directed by Brian De Palma
Screenplay: Charles Hirsch and Brian De Palma. *Producer*: Charles Hirsch. *Director of Photography*: Robert Fiore. *Editor*: Brian De Palma.

Sound: Charles Ritts and Jeffrey Lesser. *Music*: The Children of Paradise. *Costumes*: Chuck Shields (Pseudonym for Charles Hirsch)
A West End Film. Released by Sigma III
Color. Running time: 88 minutes. Shot in New York City and Secaucus, New Jersey. Rated 'X'.

Starring: Robert De Niro (Jon Rubin), Jonathan Worden (Paul Shaw), Gerrit Graham (Lloyd Clay), Allen Garfield (Porno Merchant), Ted Lescault (Bookstore Manager), Rutanya Alda (Linda), Tisa Chiang (Vietnamese Girl), Jack Cowley (Photographer), Bettina Kugel (Tina), Megan McCormick (Marina), Richard Landis (Ex-G.I.), Ray Tuttle (Television News Correspondent), Ashley Oliver (Bronx Secretary), Carol Patton (Blonde at Party and Park), Sara-Jo Edlin (Nymphomaniac).

Greetings: received the Gold Bear Award at the 1968 Berlin Film Festival.

DIONYSUS IN '69 *(1969) (Documentary)*
Directed by Brian De Palma, Robert Fiore and Bruce Rubin
Producers: Brian De Palma, Robert Fiore and Bruce Rubin in association with the Performance Group. *Directors of Photography*: Brian De Palma and Robert Fiore. *Editing*: Brian De Palma and Bruce Rubin.
Sound: Bruce Rubin. *Mixing*: Jim Townsend.
Released by Sigma III.
Black and white. Running time: 90 minutes. Shot at the Performing Garage, New York. Rated X

Starring: The Performance Group: William Finley (Dionysus), William Shepard (Penthee), Joan McIntosh (Agave), Samuel Blazer (Coryphee), John Bousseau, Richard Dic, Vickie May, Patrick McDermott, Margaret Ryan, Ciel Smith.

HI, MOM! *(1970)*
Directed by Brian De Palma
Screenplay: Brian De Palma. *Story*: Brian De Palma and Charles Hirsch.
Producer: Charles Hirsch. *Director of Photography*: Robert Elfstrom.
Editor: Paul Hirsch. *Music*: Eric Kaz. *Songs*: "Hi, Mom!" written by John Andreolli, sung by Jeffrey Lesser, "I'm Looking For You," written by John Andreolli, sung by Boney Srabian, "Be Black Baby,"

written by John Andreolli, sung by Grady Tate. *Art Direction*: Peter
Bocour. *Still Photography*: Bart De Palma and Joseph Consentino.
A West End Film. Released by Sigma III.
Black and white and color. Running time: 87 minutes. Shot in New
York City. Rated R.

Starring: Robert De Niro (Jon Rubin), Allen Garfield (Joe Banner), Jennifer
Salt (Judy Bishop), Lara Parker (Jeannie Mitchell), Gerrit Graham (Gerrit
Wood), Charles Durnham [who later changed his name to Charles Durning],
(The Superintendent), Peter Maloney (Pharmacist), Floyd Peterson (Journal-
ist); with Rutanya Alda, Beth Bowden, Gene Elman, Joe Fields, Paul Milvy,
Joe Stillman, Carol Vogel ("Be Black Baby," the Audience), and Buddy
Butler, David Connell, Milton Earl Forrest, Carolyn Craven, Joyce Griffin,
Kirk Kerksey ("Be Black Baby," the Troupe).

GET TO KNOW YOUR RABBIT *(1970, released in 1972)*
Directed by Brian De Palma
Screenplay: Jordan Crittenden. *Producers*: Steve Bernhardt and Paul
Gaer. *Executive Producer*: Peter Nelson. *Associate Producer*: Robert
Birnbaum. *Director of Photography*: John Alonzo. *Editor*: Peter Colbert.
Music: Jack Elliott and Allyn Ferguson. *Art Direction*: William Malley.
Costumes: Wayne Reed. *Magic Adviser*: Harry Blackstone Jr.
Released by Warner Brothers
Color. Running time: 93 minutes. Shot in California. Rated R.

Starring: Tom Smothers (Donald Beeman), John Astin (Mr. Turnbull),
Katharine Ross (The Terrific-Looking Girl), Orson Welles (Mr. Delasandro),
Allen Garfield (Vic), Hope Summers (Ms. Beeman), M. Emmet Walsh (Mr.
Wendel), Suzanne Zenor (Paula), Samantha Jones (Susan), Jack Collins (Mr.
Reese), Helen Page Camp (Mrs. Wendel), Charles Lane (Mr. Beeman).

SISTERS *(Blood Sisters* in England) *(1973)*
Directed by Brian De Palma
Screenplay: Brian De Palma and Louisa Rose. *Story*: Brian De Palma.
Producer: Edward R. Pressman. *Associate Producers*: Lynn Pressman
and Robert Rohdie. *Production Supervisor*: Louis A. Stroller. *Director
of Photography*: Gregory Sandor. *Editor*: Paul Hirsch. *Music*: Bernard
Herrmann. *Sound*: Russell Arthur. *Sound Editor*: John Fox. *Music*

Editor: Robert Hathaway. *Mixing*: Dick Vorisek. *Production Designer*:
Gary Weist. *Opening Credits created by*: Richard Hess. *Researcher*:
Jay Cocks
A Pressman-Williams Production. Released by American International
Pictures
Color and black and white. Running time: 93 minutes. Shot in Manhat-
tan and Staten Island, New York. Rated R.

Starring: Margot Kidder (Danielle Blanchion-Breton), Jennifer Salt (Grace
Collier), Charles Durning (Joseph Larch), William Finley (Emil Breton),
Lisle Wilson (Philip Woode), Mary Davenport (Mrs. Collier), Bernard
Hughes (Arthur McLennen), Dolph Sweet (Detective Kelly).
Sisters was honored at the 1973 Dallas Film Festival. Margot Kidder received
the award for best actress and Bernard Herrmann for best music at the 1973
Atlanta Film Festival.

PHANTOM OF THE PARADISE (1974)
Directed by Brian De Palma
Screenplay: Brian De Palma. *Producer*: Edward R. Pressman. *Executive
Producer*: Gustave Berne. *Associate Producers*: Paul Lewis, Bill Scott,
Jeffrey Hayes, and Michael Arciaga. *Director of Photography*: Larry
Pizer. *Editor*: Paul Hirsch. *Sound*: James Tanenbaum. *Sound Editors*:
Dan Sable and Harriet Glickenstein. *Music and Songs*: Paul Williams.
Additional Music: George Aliceson Tipton. *Music Supervisors*: Michael
Arciaga and Jules Chaikin. *Songs*: "Goodbye, Eddie, Goodbye," per-
formed by The Juicy Fruits, lead vocal: Archie Hahn, "Faust," vocal:
William Finley, "Upholstery," performed by The Beach Bums, lead voc-
al: Jeffrey Comanor, "Special to Me" (Phoenix Audition Song), vocal:
Jessica Harper, "Phantom's Theme (The Beauty and The Beast), vocal:
Paul Williams, "Somebody Super Like You" (Beef Construction Song),
performed by The Undead, lead vocal: Harold Oblong, "Life at Last,"
lead vocal Ray Kennedy, "Old Souls," vocal: Jessica Harper, "The Hell
of It," vocal: Paul Williams. *Music Editor*: Ed Norton. *Mixing*: Al
Gramaglia, Magno Sound, Inc. *Special Effects*: Greg Auer. *Special Visual Effects* (Wedding Sequence): Robert Elfstrom and James Signorelli.
Choreography: Harold Oblong. *Choreography* (Wedding Sequence): William Shepard. *Set Decorators*: Jack Fisk and Sissy Spacek. *Costumes*:
Rosanna Norton
A Pressman-Williams Production. Released by Twentieth Century Fox.

Color. Running time: 91 minutes. Shot in New York, Los Angeles and Dallas. Rated R.

Starring: Paul Williams (Swan), William Finley (Winslow Leach), Jessica Harper (Phoenix), Gerrit Graham (Beef), George Memmoli (Harold Philbin). *Phantom of the Paradise* received the Grand Prize at the Avoriaz (France) Film Festival in 1974. The Academy Awards nominated *Phantom* in the Best Original Score.

OBSESSION (1976)
Directed by Brian De Palma
Screenplay: Paul Schrader and Brian De Palma. *Story*: Brian De Palma. *Producers*: George Litto and Harry Blum. *Executive Producer*: Robert S. Bremson. *Director of Photography*: Vilmos Zsigmond. *Editor*: Paul Hirsch. *Sound Editor*: Dan Sable. *Sound Mixer*: David Ronne. *Music*: Bernard Herrmann, performed by the National Philharmonic (London) and The Thames Choir. *Art Direction*: Jack Senter. *Visual Consultant*: Anne Pritchard. *Portrait Paintings*: Barton De Palma.
Released by Columbia Pictures
Color. Running time: 98 minutes. Shot in Florence, Italy and in New Orleans. Rated PG.

Starring: Cliff Robertson (Michael Courtland), Genevieve Bujold (Elizabeth Courtland/Amy Courtland = Sandra Portinari), John Lithgow (Robert La Salle), Wanda Blackman (Amy Courtland as a little girl), Sylvia Williams (Judy), Patrick McNamara (Kidnapper), Stanley J. Reeves (Inspector Brie), Stocker Fontelieu (Dr. Ellman), Nella Simoncini Barbieri (Mrs. Portinari), Tom Felleghy (Italian Businessman), Don Hood (Ferguson), Regis Cordic (Journalist), John Creamer (Policeman).
Obsession was nominated for Best Original Score at the 1976 Academy Awards.

CARRIE (1976)
Directed by Brian De Palma
Screenplay: Lawrence D. Cohen, based on the novel by Stephen King. *Producer*: Paul Monash. *Associate Producer*: Louis A. Stroller. *Director of Photography*: Mario Tosi. *Editing*: Paul Hirsch. *Music Composed by*: Pino Donaggio. *Music Conducted by*: Natale Massara. *Song*: "I Never Dreamed Someone Like You Could Want Someone Like Me" and

"Born to Have It All," sung by Katie Irving, lyrics by Merrit Malloy.
Sound Editing: Dan Sable. *Sound Mixer*: Bertil Jalberg. *Art Direction*:
Jack Fisk and William Kenny. *Special Effects*: Gregory M. Auer. *Stunts*:
Richard Weiker. *Costume Designer*: Rosanna Norton.
Released by United Artists
Color. Running Time: 98 minutes. Shot in Los Angeles. Rated R.

Starring: Sissy Spacek (Carrie White), Piper Laurie (Margaret White), Amy
Irving (Sue Snell), William Katt (Tommy Ross), John Travolta (Billy Nolan),
Nancy Allen (Chris Hargenson), Betty Buckley (Miss Collins, the Gym
Teacher), Priscilla Pointer (Miss Snell), P.J. Soles (Norma Watson), Michael
Talbot (Freddy), Doug Cox ("The Beak," the Class Photographer), Harry
Gold (George), Noelle North (Frieda), Cibdy Daly (Cora), Edie McClurg
(Helen), Rory Stevens (Kenny), Anson Downes (Ernest), Deirdre Bethrong
(Rhonda), Cameron De Palma (Boy on Bicycle).
Carrie received the Grand Prize at the 1976 Avoriaz (France) Film Festival.
Sissy Spacek received a nomination for Best Actress and Piper Laurie for Best
Supporting Actress at the 1976 Academy Awards. Sissy Spacek won the 1976
Best Actress at the National Film Critics Circle Award.
Carrie became a Broadway musical in 1988, directed by Terry Hands, book
by Lawrence D. Cohen, Music by Michael Gore, Lyrics by Dean Pitchford,
starring Betty Buckley, Darlene Love, Gene Anthony Ray.

THE FURY (1978)
Directed by Brian De Palma
Screenplay: John Farris, based on his novel. *Producer*: Frank Yablans.
Executive Producer: Ron Preissman. *Associate Producer*: Jack B. Bern-
stein. *Director of Photography*: Richard H. Kline. *Editor*: Paul Hirsch.
Sound Editor: Dan Sable. *Music*: John Williams. *Art Direction*: Richard
Lawrence. *Set Designer*: Bill Malley. *Special Effects*: A. D. Flowers.
Special Make-up Effects Supervisor: William Tuttle. *Special Make-up
Effects*: Rick Baker. *Assistant Special Make-up Effects*: Rob Bottin. *Cos-
tume Designer*: Theoni V. Aldredge
Released by Twentieth Century Fox
Color. Running Time: 118 Minutes. Shot in Chicago, California (special
effects) and Israel. Rated R.

Starring: Kirk Douglas (Peter Sandza), John Cassavetes (Childress), Amy
Irving (Gillian Bellaver), Carrie Snodgrass (Hester), Andrew Stevens (Robin
Sandza), Charles Durning (Dr. Jim McKeever), Fiona Lewis (Susan Charles),
Carol Rossen (Dr. Ellen Linstrom), Joyce Easton (Mrs. Bellaver), William

Finley (Raymond Dunwoode), Rutanya Alda (Kristen), Jane Lambert (Vivian Nuckells), J. Patrick McNamara (Robertson), Dennis Franz (Bob, the Policeman), Darryl Hannah (Pam), Melodie Thomas (Gillian's friend).

HOME MOVIES (1980)
Directed by Brian De Palma
Screenplay: Robert Harders, Gloria Norris, Kim Ambler, Dana Edelman, Stephen Lemay, and Charles Loventhal. *Story*: Brian De Palma. *Producers*: Brian De Palma, Jack Temchin, and Gil Adler. *Executive Producers*: Sam Irvin and Mark Rosman. *Director of Photography*: James L. Carter. *Editor*: Corky O'Hara. *Editing Supervisor*: Paul Hirsch. *Sound*: Rick Wadell. *Music Composed by*: Pino Donaggio. *Music Conducted by*: Natale Massara. *Art Direction*: Tom Surgal. *Animated Titles*: Howard Danelowitz.
An SLM Film. Released by United Artists Classics. Color. Running Time: 90 minutes. Shot at Sarah Lawrence College and in Connecticut. Rated PG.

Starring: Kirk Douglas (Dr. Tuttle, The Maestro), Nancy Allen (Kristina), Keith Gordon (Dennis Byrd), Gerrit Graham (James Byrd), Vincent Gardenia (Dr. Byrd), Mary Davenport (Mrs. Byrd), Captain Haggerty (Officer Quinn), Loretta Tupper (Grandma), Charles Loventhal (Thomas), Jeff Graham (Luke), Bunny (Bunny).

DRESSED TO KILL (1980)
Directed by Brian De Palma.
Screenplay: Brian De Palma. *Producers*: George Litto. *Associate Producer*: Fred Caruso. *Director of Photography*: Ralph Bode. *Editor*: Jerry Greenberg. *Sound Editor*: Dan Sable. *Sound*: John Bolz. *Music Composed by*: Pino Donaggio. *Music Conducted by*: Natale Massara. *Set Decorator*: Gary Weist. *Costumes*: Ann Roth. *Costume Designer*: Gary Jones.
A Samuel Z. Arkoff Presentation. Released by Filmways Pictures Cinemascope. Color. Running Time: 105 minutes. Shot in New York and Philadelphia (museum sequence; interiors only). Rated R.

Starring: Michael Caine (Dr. Robert Elliott), Angie Dickinson (Kate Miller), Nancy Allen (Liz Blake), Keith Gordon (Peter Miller), Dennis Franz (Detective Marino), David Margulies (Dr. Levy), Ken Baker (Warren Lockman, the Man at the Museum), Brandon Maggart (Cleveland Sam),

Susanna Clemm (Miss Luce and Bobbi), Fred Weber (Mike Miller), Bill Randolph (Cab Driver, Chase Sequence), Sean O'Rinn (Cab Driver, Lovemaking Sequence), Robert Lee Rush (Hood, Subway Sequence), Mary Davenport (Woman in the Restaurant), Anneka De Lorenzo (Nurse, Asylum), Robbie L. McDermott (Man in the Shower).

BLOW OUT *(1981)*
Directed by Brian De Palma
Screenplay: Brian De Palma. *Producer*: George Litto. *Executive Producer and Production Manager*: Fred Caruso *Director of Photography*: Vilmos Zsigmond. *Editor*: Paul Hirsch. *Sound* (Dolby): Jim Tannenbaum. *Music Composed by*: Pino Donaggio. *Music Conducted by*: Natale Massara. *Production Designer*: Paul Sylbert. *Set Designer*: Jeannie Oppewell. *Underwater Cameraman*: Rex Metz. *Costume Designer*: Vicki Sanchez. *Nancy Allen's Costumes Designed by*: Ann Roth
A Cinema 77, Geria Films Production. Released by Filmways Pictures Cinemascope, Color. Running Time: 107 minutes. Shot in Philadelphia and Hollywood (underwater sequence and John Lithgow's death). Rated R.

Starring: John Travolta (Jack Terri), Nancy Allen (Sally Bedina), John Lithgow (Burke), Dennis Franz (Manny Karp), Peter Boyden (Sam), Curt May (Frank Donohue), Ernest McClure (Jim), Dave Roberts (Anchor Man), Maurice Copeland (Jack Manners), John Aquino (Detective), John Hoffmeister (McRyan), Patrick McNamara (Officer Nelson), Terence Currier (Lawrence Henry), Tom McCarthy (Policeman), Dean Bennett (Campus Guard).

SCARFACE *(1983)*
Directed by Brian De Palma
Screenplay: Oliver Stone. *Producer*: Martin Bregman *Executive Producer*: Louis A. Stroller. *Director of Photography*: John A. Alonzo. *Editor*: Jerry Greenberg and David Ray. *Sound*: Charles Darin Knight. *Music*: Giorgio Moroder. *Art Direction*: Ed Richardson. *Costumes*: Patricia Norris
Released by Universal Pictures
Color. Running Time: 106 minutes. Shot in Florida. Dedicated to Howard Hawks and Ben Hecht. Rated R.

Starring: Al Pacino (Tony Montana), Steven Bauer (Manny Ray), Michele Pfeiffer (Elvira), Mary Elizabeth Mastrantonio (Gina), Robert Loggia

(Lopez), F. Murray Abraham (Omar), Paul Shenar (Alejandro Sosa), Al Israel (Hector, The Toad), Miriam Colon (Mama Montana), Gregg Henry (Politician from Washington).

BODY DOUBLE *(1984)*

Directed by Brian De Palma. *Screenplay*: Robert J. Avrech and Brian De Palma. *Story*: Brian De Palma. *Producer*: Brian De Palma. *Executive Producer*: Howard Gottfried. *Director of Photography*: Stephen H. Burum. *Editor*: Jerry Greenberg and Bill Pankow. *Sound*: James Tannenbaum. *Music Composed by*: Pino Donaggio. *Music Conducted by*: Natale Massara. *Songs*: "Relax," performed by Frankie Goes to Hollywood, Courtesy of ZTT/Island Records, Inc., "The House Is Burning" (video clip), performed by Vivabeat, Courtesy of Derek Khan Chang and Vivabeat. *Production Designer*: Ida Random. *Costume Designer*: Gloria Gersham. *Special Make-up for the Indian*: Tom Burman and Bari Dreiband
Released by Columbia Pictures
Color. Dolby. Running Time: 114 minutes. Shot in Hollywood. Rated R.

Starring: Craig Wasson (Jake Scully), Melanie Griffith (Holly Body), Gregg Henry (Sam Bouchard. Richard Revelle. The Indian), Deborah Shelton (Gloria Revelle), Guy Boyd (Detective Jim McLean), Dennis Franz (Rubin, the Director), David Haskell (Drama Teacher), Al Israel (Corso, the Porno Film Producer), Rebecca Stanley (Kimberley).

WISE GUYS *(1986)*

Directed by Brian De Palma
Screenplay: George Gallo and Norman Steinberg (only Gallo received a screen credit). *Producer*: Aaron Russo. *Associate Producer*: Patrick McCormick. *Executive Producer*: Irwin Russo. *Director of Photography*: Fred Schuler. *Editor*: Jerry Greenberg. *Sound*: Les Lazarowitz. *Sound Editor*: Dan Sable. *Music*: Ira Newborn. *Song*: "Pink Cadillac," performed by Bruce Springsteen, Courtesy of CBS Records. *Production Designer*: Edward Pisoni. *Costume Designer*: Richard Bruno
Released by Metro Goldwyn Mayer/United Artists
Color. Running Time: 91 minutes. Shot in New Jersey. Rated PG.

Starring: Danny DeVito (Harry Valentini), Joe Piscopo (Moe Dickstein), Harvey Keitel (Bobby DiLea), Ray Scharkey (Marco), Dan Hedaya (Anthony Castelo), Captain Lou Albano (Frank "the Fixer" Acavano), Julie Bovasso (Lil Dickstein), Patti LuPone (Wanda Valentini), Antonia Rey (Aunt Sadie), Mimi Cecchini (Grandma Valentini).

THE UNTOUCHABLES *(1987)*
Directed by Brian De Palma
Screenplay: David Mamet. *Producer*: Art Linson. *Director of Photography*: Stephen H. Burum. *Editor*: Jerry Greenberg and Bill Pankow. *Sound*: Jim Tannenbaum. *Sound Editing*: Dan Sable. *Music*: Ennio Morricone. *Art Direction*: William A. Elliott. *Visual Consultant*: Patrizia Von Brandenstein. *Set Decoration*: Hal Gausman. *Set Design*: E. C. Chen, Steven P. Sardanis, Gil Clayton, Nicholas Laborczy. *Costume Designer*: Marilyn Vance. *Costumes*: Giorgio Armani. *Stunts*: Gary Hymes. Released by Paramount Pictures
Cinemascope. Color. Dolby. Running Time: 119 minutes. Shot in Chicago. Rated R.

Starring: Kevin Costner (Eliot Ness), Sean Connery (James Malone), Charles Martin Smith (Oscar Wallace), Andy Garcia (George Stone), Robert De Niro (Al Capone), Richard Bradford (Mike), Jack Kehoe (Walter Payne), Brad Sullivan (George), Patricia Clakson (Catherine Ness), Billy Drago (Frank Nitti).
Ennio Morricone won a Grammy Award for Best Film Score. Sean Connery received the Golden Globe Award and the Academy Award for Best Supporting Actor. *The Untouchables* received the following Academy Award Nominations: Best Music (Ennio Morricone), Best Costume Designer (Marilyn Vance), Best Achievement in Art Director (Patrizia Von Brandenstein), Art Direction (William A. Elliott), Set Decoration (Hal Gausman).

CASUALTIES OF WAR *(1988)*
Directed by Brian De Palma
Screenplay: David Rabe, based on a novel by David Lang. *Producer*: Art Linson. *Director of Photography*: Stephen H. Burum. *Editor*: Bill Pankow. Released by Columbia Pictures
Shot in Thailand.

Starring: Michael J. Fox, Sean Penn

Nonfiction Books

Joseph Gelmis. *The Film Director As A Superstar*. London:Secker & Warburg, 1970.

The Performance Group. *Dionysus in '69*. New York:Farrar, Straus & Giroux, 1970.

Michael Pye and Linda Myles. *The Movie Brats*. New York:Holt, Rinehart & Winston, 1979.

James Monaco. *American Film Now*. New York:NAL/Plume, 1979.

David Pirie. *Anatomy of the Movies*. London:Windward, 1981.

David Thompson. *Overexposures*. New York:William Morrow & Co., 1981.

Stephen King. *Danse Macabre*. New York:Everest House/Berkley, 1981.

Michael Bliss. *Brian De Palma*. London:Scarecrow Press, 1983.

Jean Pierre Coursodon with Pierre Sauvage. *American Directors, Volume II*. New York:McGraw-Hill, 1983.

Dale Pollock. *Skywalking*. New York:Harmony, 1983.

Douglas E. Winter. *Stephen King, the Art of Darkness*. New York:NAL Books, 1984.

Susan Dworkin. *Double De Palma*. New York:Newmarket Press, 1984.

John McCarty. *Splatter Movies*. New York:Saint Martin's Press, 1984.

Note: Arrangement of works is by date of publication.

William Schoell. *Stay out of the Shower*. New York:Dembner Books, 1985.

Pauline Kael. *State of the Art*. New York:EP Dutton, 1985.

Joel W. Finler, *The Movie Directors Story*. Crescent, 1985.

John McCarty. *Psychos*. New York:Saint Martin's Press, 1986.

Jessie Horsting. *Stephen King at the Movies*. New York:NAL/Signet, 1986.

Robin Wood. *From Vietnam to Hollywood*. New York:Columbia University Press, 1986.

Martin Amis. *The Moronic Inferno and Other Visits to America*. New York:Viking Penguin, 1987.

Jeff Corner. *Stephen King Goes to Hollywood*. New York:NAL/Plume, 1987.

Krin Gabbard and Glen O. Gabbard. *Psychiatry in the Cinema*. Chicago:University of Chicago Press, 1987.

Leonard Maltin. *TV Movies and Video Guide*. New York:NAL/Signet, 1987.

Gregory A. Waller, Editor. *American Horrors, Essays on the Modern American Horror Films*. Champaign:University of Illinois Press, 1987.

Molly Haskell. *From Reverence to Rape, the Treatment of Women in the Movies*, 2nd ed. Chicago:University of Chicago Press, 1987.

The Untouchables: The Official Movie Magazine. New York:NAL/Signet, 1987.

NOVELS

Daniel Lang. *Casualties of War*. New York:McGraw-Hill, 1969.

Gerald Walker. *Cruising*. Briarcliff Manor, N.Y.:Stein and Day, 1970.

Bjarne Rostaing. *Phantom of the Paradise*. New York:Dell, 1975.

Stephen King. *Carrie*. New York:Doubleday & Co., 1974.

John Farris. *The Fury*. New York:Tor Books, 1977.

Brian De Palma and Campbell Black. *Dressed to Kill*. New York:Bantam, 1980.

Neal Williams. *Blow Out*. New York:Bantam, 1981.

Paul Monette. *Scarface*. New York:Berkley, 1983.

Marvin Albert. *The Untouchables*. New York:Ivy Books, 1987.

Eliot Ness with Oscar Fraley. *The Untouchables*. 1957. Reprint. New York:Pocket Books, 1987.

INTERVIEWS
Conducted by Laurent Bouzereau

"Body Double." Interviews with Craig Wasson and Melanie Griffith. *L'ecran fantastique*, March 1985.

"Oliver Stone." Interview with Oliver Stone. *Globe*, April 1986.

"Edward R. Pressman." Interview with Ed Pressman. *L'Ecran fantastique*, May 1986.

"Brian De Palma in '86." Interview with Brian De Palma. *L'Ecran Fantastique*, September 1986.

"Nancy Allen." Interview with Nancy Allen. *L'Ecran Fantastique*, December 1986.

"Ken Wiederhorn." Interview with Ken Wiederhorn. *L'Ecran Fantastique*, July 1987.

"Kevin Costner." Interview with Kevin Costner. *Globe*, October 1987.

ARTICLES

"The Wedding Party." *Filmfacts*, 1969.

William Bayer. "Was That Any Way to Greet *Greetings*?" *New York Times*, January 12, 1969.

Robin Wood. "Sisters." *American Nightmares*, 1979.

Brian De Palma. "Murder by Moog, Scoring the Chill." *Village Voice*, October 11, 1973.

David Bartholomew. "De Palma of the Paradise." *Cinefantastique*, 1974.

Mike Childs and Alan Jones. "De Palma Has the Power." *Cinefantastique*, Summer 1977.

Roger Greenspun. "Carrie, Sally and Leatherface Among the Film Buffs." *Film Comment*, January/February 1977.

Michael Henry. "L'oeil du Malin." *Positif*, January 1977.

Tom Buckley. "Yablans Explores the Mysteries of Sneak Previews." *New York Times*, March 3, 1978.

Jennifer Dunning. "Brian De Palma: I Operate on the Principle of Escalating Terror." *New York Times*, April 23, 1978.

Sam Irvin. "*The Fury*: A Location Journal." *Cinefantastique*, 1977.

Gerald Peary. "Working His Way Through College." *Take One*, January 1977.

"Sobsession" (parody). *Mad*, June 1977.

Andrew Epstein. "Requiem for Home Movies." *Los Angeles Times*, August 2, 1980.

"The *Take One* Write a Script for Brian De Palma Contest." *Take One*, January 1979.

"Undressed to Kill" (parody). *Mad*, April 1981.

David Rosenthal. "Dressed for a Killing." *New York Magazine*, August 1981.

Serge Daney and Jonathan Rosenbaum. "Brian De Palma." *Les cahiers du cinéma*, 1981.

David Marsh. *"Blow Out,* Film of the Year." *Films of the Year*, 1981.

"Ear Witness." *Film Illustrated*, November 1981.

Kristin McMurran. "Why No Blowups on *Blow Out*? Because Travolta, Allen and De Palma Are Just Friends." *People Magazine*, August 17, 1981.

Michiko Kakutani. "Brian De Palma." *New York Times*, July 9, 1981.

Michael Mills. "Brian De Palma." *Moviegoer*, December 1983.

Georgia A. Brown. *"Obsession." American Film*, December 1983.

Lynn, Hirschberg. "Brian De Palma's Deathwish." *Esquire*, January 1984.

"Scared Face" (parody). *Mad*. July 1984.

Thomas McKlevery Cleaver. *"Scarface." American Cinematographer*, December 1984.

"20 Questions: Brian De Palma." *Playboy*, December 1983.

Marcia Rally. "Brian's Body." *Film Comment*, October 1984.

David Denby. "The Woman in the Windows." *New York Magazine*, November 5, 1984.

"Flesh and Fantasies." *Newsweek*, October 29, 1984.

Tom Hinckley. "Brian De Palma." *Cable Guide*, October 1984.

Gene Siskel. "Untouchables." *Chicago Tribune*, September 21, 1986.

Brian De Palma. "Guilty Pleasures." *Film Comment*, June 1987.

David Mamet. "I Lost It at the Movies." *American Film*, June 1987.

Jesse Kornbluth. "Shot by Shot." *Premiere*, August 1987.

Steve Pond. "The Hero's a Hired Gun." *Premiere*, August 1987.

Tom Mathews, Michael Reese, Jane Huck, Laura Shapiro, Ray Shawhill, and Jack Kroll. "The Mob at the Movies." *Newsweek*, June 22, 1987.

Fred Schruers. *"The Untouchables." Rolling Stone*, March 1987.

Kevin Lally. "Ness and Capone Clash Again in New *Untouchables* Feature." Film Journal, June 1987.

David Lila. "Bloody Brian." *Women's Wear Daily*, June 1987.

Kurt Loder. "Brian De Palma." *Rolling Stone*, December 1987.

"The Unwatchables" (parody). *Mad*, December 1987.

SCREENPLAYS

Sisters, by Brian De Palma and Louisa Rose. Copyright 1970 (revised draft February 21, 1972.

Cruising, by Brian De Palma, based on the book by Gerald Walker. Copyright 1974.

The Demolished Man, by Brian De Palma, adapted from the novel by Alfred
    Bester. Copyright March 1977.
Dressed to Kill, by Brian De Palma. Copyright 1979.
Blow Out, by Brian De Palma. Copyright 1981.
Fire, by Brian De Palma (first draft). Copyright April 14, 1982.
Scarface, by Oliver Stone (final draft). Copyright November 1, 1982.
Body Double, by Robert J. Avrech and Brian De Palma (final draft).
    Copyright October 1982.
Wise Guys, by George Gallo and Norman Steinberg. Copyright January 28,
    1985.
The Untouchables, by David Mamet. Copyright 1985, 1986.

SOUNDTRACKS

Sisters (Southern Cross Records Audiophile Records and Compact Discs)
Phantom of the Paradise (A&M Records and Tapes)
Obsession (Phase 4 Records)
Carrie (UA Records and Tapes)
The Fury (Arista Records)
Home Movies (Varese Sarabande Records)
Dressed to Kill (Varese Sarabande Records)
Blow Out (Polydor Records)
Scarface (MCA Records and Tapes)
The Untouchables (A&M Records, Tapes, and Compact Discs)

DE PALMA ON VIDEO

The Wedding Party (Vidamerica)
Sisters (Warner)
Phantom of the Paradise (Key Video)
Obsession (RCA/Columbia)
Carrie (CBS/Fox)
The Fury (CBS/Fox)
Home Movies (Vestron)
Dressed to Kill (Warner)
Blow Out (Warner)
Scarface (MCA)
Body Double (RCA/Columbia)
Wise Guys (MGM)
The Untouchables (Paramount)

INDEX

DATE DUE

The Library Store   #47-0103